IN SEARCH OF
Secret
Suffolk

A Souvenir and Guide to Suffolk

Robert Leader

THOROGOOD

Published by Thorogood
10-12 Rivington Street
London EC2A 3DU

Telephone: 020 7749 4748
Fax: 020 7729 6110
Email: info@thorogood.ws
Web: www.thorogood.ws

Thorogood is a publishing division
of Acorn Magazines

A CIP catalogue record for this book is available
from the British Library.

ISBN 1 85418 209 9

Printed in India by Replika Press Pvt. Ltd.

Designed by Driftdesign

FOREWORD

The chapters in this book all originated as photo-features in the Suffolk Journal. They represent four years of wandering with a camera through the byways and villages, the towns and the riverbanks, the countryside and the seashore, of one of the most beautiful counties of England. There are no spectacular peaks, or lakes, or mountains here, instead the beauty of Suffolk is of a more gentle kind; the pastoral charm that Constable knew so well, the rose-wreathed, pink-walled and yellow-thatched cottages drowning in overgrown gardens of flowers, the sheltered, gull-wheeling haunts of sailors and fishermen, those lovely old flint churches, and the secret walks and beauty spots where farmland and woodland meet under those soaring Suffolk skies.

There is history here, in the splendid castles, guildhalls and abbeys, and at first I explored all of those. Then I began to explore the rivers, the avenues of early exploration, and later the commercial highways of mediaeval trade. To interest a county magazine, and a discerning readership who already knew all the obvious sights and stories, it was always necessary to go a little deeper, to link what was generally known with aspects and insights into something new. I was literally *In Search Of Secret Suffolk*, and slowly it dawned upon me that I had both the title and the material for a book.

Robert Leader

CONTENTS

LIST OF ILLUSTRATIONS

Chapter seven

Chapter eight

Chapter nine

Chapter thirteen

Chapter fourteen

Chapter fifteen

Chapter sixteen

Chapter seventeen

THE LOVELY LARK –
SUFFOLK'S GENTLE RIVER

1

1 THE LOVELY LARK – SUFFOLK'S GENTLE RIVER

The River Lark rises shyly in a meandering stream through the rich Suffolk farmlands a few miles south of Bury St. Edmunds, and makes its first really public appearance when it enters the ancient grounds of what is now the Abbey Gardens. Here it flows past massive flint ruins, children's playgrounds and sumptuous flower beds, where there was once the magnificent Shrine of a King, and the Cradle of the Law.

THE IDYLLIC LARK AS IT FLOWS THROUGH THE ABBEY GARDENS IN BURY ST. EDMUNDS

The King was the young King Edmund, a blonde-haired, blue-eyed Saxon Prince, born in Germany, who was crowned King of East Anglia on Christmas Day in the year 856 AD. A devoted Christian he was, by all accounts, a much-loved and benevolent ruler, but he inherited a kingdom plagued by rampaging Norsemen who had learned that there was rich plunder to be found by sailing their armies across the North Sea to the less wild shores of England.

Raiding the rich monastery at Lindisfarne in Northumbria had given the Viking raiders a taste for English ecclesiastical treasures. The raids spread to the south of England, and within ten years of Edmund mounting his peaceful throne the warring Danes were at the borders of his East Anglian kingdom. A full-scale Danish army landed in the north and marched southward, looting, killing and burning monasteries as they went. Edmund's army tried to stop them in a savage and bloody battle at Thetford, but the Danes were fiercely triumphant. Edmund's forces were smashed and the young king was forced to flee.

Captured by the Danes, Edmund was offered a stark choice. If he would renounce his Christian faith, then they would spare his life. Edmund refused the offer, and was shot through with arrows. His head was cut off and callously thrown into a thicket. So King Edmund became Saint Edmund, the martyr.

The saint's head was later found, so the legend says, guarded by a wolf. The head was gently laid in the same grave as the murdered king's body, and a simple wooden chapel was built over the spot. Later still it was decided that this was not enough, and so the martyred remains were brought back to Bury, then called Beodricksworth, and placed more reverently in the monastery there. Soon the site became a place of regular pilgrimage, and the great Abbey of St. Edmundsbury arose to become truly The Shrine of a King, and one of the greatest and richest religious centres of mediaeval England.

ST. EDMUND, THE
MARTYR, IN THE
ABBEY GARDENS

Because the Shrine was a magnet for pilgrims, and also because it was far enough removed from London to be safe from the King's spies, the Abbey of St. Edmundsbury became, on the 20th of November in the year 1214, the secret meeting place for the barons and earls who had tired of the despotic behaviour of their arrogant King John. Twenty-five of the most powerful men in the land assembled before the High Altar, ostensibly to perform their religious duties as part of their pilgrimage on St.

Edmund's Day, but also to swear on their sacred oath, here in this Holy Place, that they would force their King to recognise and sign the Great Charter of Liberties that the Archbishop of Canterbury now presented before them.

The Great Act, or Magna Carta as it became known, set up the principles of British law, and the basic foundations for representative and constitutional government. True to their oath the barons forced the recalcitrant King John to set his seal to the charter at Runymede in June of the following year. So the Shrine of the Martyred King, had also become The Cradle of the Law.

Now the splendid Abbey and its centuries of glory have collapsed into ruins, but on the eroded bulk of one of the great flint pillars that still stands erect, two white stone tablets mark the spot where the barons gathered to make history; one lists the proud names of the twenty-five men appointed to enforce the observance of the Magna Carta, the other describes in verse how – 'Freedom, unforgetful still recites, this second birthplace of our native rights.'

The Majestic Abbey Gate, and the only slightly less imposing Norman Tower, are the only remaining parts of the Abbey not now in ruins. The Abbey Gate was erected in 1347 to replace an original destroyed by a mob of angry townspeople some twenty years before. The second time around the builders took no chances, making a solid defensive barrier for the Great Abbey, complete with archer stations and a massive portcullis.

Look up at the Abbey Gate and then let your eye travel right to the glorious fifteenth century facade of St. James Cathedral, very soon to have a brand new cathedral tower. Inside are glorious stained glass windows, and a magnificent ceiling where the hammerbeams terminate in angels and shields. The Abbey Gateway and the Cathedral face on to the Angel Hill, once the site of the annual Bury Fair, and overlooked on the opposite side by the Angel Hotel, the old creeper-covered coaching inn where Charles Dickens, and his famous Samuel Pickwick, both stayed, one in fact and the other in fiction.

At the top of Abbeygate Street is the old Corn Exchange, looking more like some transplanted Greek temple with its huge portico of Doric columns, and above them a splendidly decorated triangular gable. In the centre of the gable design is the head of Queen Victoria and on either side of her are a young Adonis with a plough and oxen and a beautiful young woman bearing corn sheaves.

THE MAGNIFICENT GRECIAN FRONTAGE OF BURY'S CORN EXCHANGE

Close by is the diminutive Nutshell, claimed as the smallest pub in England. A few steps further and you are into the Butter-market, so named because in mediaeval days the local farmers sold their butter here, along with a whole range of farm animals and other produce. At the top end of the market stands the Moyses Hall Museum, a solid flint and brick building which looks like an ancient church with its wooden tower and tiled spire. However, it was built as a 12th Century merchant's house, which makes it the oldest building in Bury. Inside, its cavernous ground storey is vaulted between massive arches that now divide the exhibitions of local archaeology and history.

Also overlooking the top end of the Buttermarket are the handsome columns and triangular gables of the Market Cross, which was originally constructed as a playhouse in 1771. Later it became the Town Hall, and now its upper storey contains the town's art gallery. However, the old trademark masks of Comedy and Tragedy can still be seen in the carved panels on the outer walls.

Almost facing the Market Cross is the beautiful neo-Jacobean shopfront that is now a branch of W.H. Smith. It was built for Boots the Chemists in the mid 19th Century, and the whole frontage is well worth a second look. Framed in its carved black timbers are niches containing the white statues of four English Kings, including St. Edmund, while the top central, black-edged gable frames a stucco relief of the seated King and Saint.

Leading north from the top corner of the Buttermarket is St. John's Street. Like all the delightful old streets of Bury it winds between character filled shops and buildings where no two roofs are at the same level. Half way down are the soaring stone spires of the magnificent Church of St. John The Evangelist. There are nine of them in a tight cluster, eight small ones ascending four by four to the topmost spire which pierces upwards in a veritable spear thrust straight to heaven. That formidable central spire is the highest landmark in the town of Bury.

BURY ST. EDMUNDS,
THE SPLENDID
SPIRE OF ST. JOHN'S
CHURCH

A few miles south-west of Bury is Ickworth Park, containing one of the brightest jewels of the National Trust, Ickworth House, an Italiante marvel with its immense rotunda soaring high above the elegant , palatial wings curving away on either side. Its columns and the friezes depicting the stories of the Iliad and the Odyssey, are a glory of architectural detail. The house, now owned by the National Trust, was the ancestral home of the Bristol family and its ambitious design was started by the Fourth Earl in 1795 as a showcase for his magnificent collections of European art.

THE ROTUNDA OF ICKWORTH HOUSE

Set in magnificent parkland where sheep graze under mighty oaks, the grounds contain many fine walks, a small, breeze-rippled lake, a summerhouse, a vineyard, a private family church, and a deer park, where haughty stags parade before their harems. The house itself is a treasure store of beautiful sculptures, paintings and objects' d'art too numerous to list. If the Vikings were still raiding East Anglia, then Ickworth House would have to be one of their first targets for superlative plunder.

In Spring the grounds of Ickworth are ablaze with golden daffodils; but to really see daffodils in solid yellow rivers, almost a mile long like a divided yellow sea, you have to visit Nowton Park, another two hundred acres of landscaped woodland walks and playing fields which is just south of Bury.

Proud parents bring their children here over Easter to play and be photographed against the golden backdrop. The surrounding woodlands include mighty cedars, redwoods and copper beeches, all broken up with small ponds, a lake and wildflower meadows.

But we are straying from the Lark, which makes its exit from the north side of the Abbey Gardens beneath the Abbot's Bridge, a buttressed three-arch flint bridge which was part of the old abbey walls. Flowing out of town parallel to Fornham Road, the gentle river winds its lazy way through the green swards of Fornham St. Martin Golf Course, and then, in Spring, ducks out of sight again under curtains of white blossom behind the Fornham St. Martin to Fornham All Saints road. There is a shady footpath for the energetic to follow its course, but the average car driver will pick it up again as it flows by the West Stow Country Park some five miles further on.

Here at West Stow you can walk part of the old tow path, where horse and pony drawn shallow barges once carried coal, grain and timber, as far upstream as Bury St. Edmunds. In those seventeenth-century days, when the rural roads were little more than cart tracks, many enterprising farms and businesses had their own private wharves along the river. Now the river traffic is no more, and the Lark flows peacefully over trailing reed beds and shallows, the home of drifting swans, geese and mallard.

It was the river which brought the Anglo-Saxons to West Stow, where they settled soon after the Romans had departed around 450 AD. Here archaeologists have uncovered the site of one of their early villages, which has now been reconstructed, using as near as possible the same tools and techniques that would have been used in the fifth century.

THE RE-CREATED ANGLO-SAXON VILLAGE AT WEST STOW

The original post holes were discovered, and were used to help determine the positions, shape and structure of the original buildings, and then to support the timbers of the new reconstructions. The thatch-roofed post houses, built over sunken pits, are supplemented by a modern Visitor Centre and an exhibition of early tools and techniques, and there are regular open days when costumed 'Saxons' give craft demonstrations and colourful glimpses of Saxon village life as it probably was fifteen hundred years ago. To add to the authenticity even the coarse-haired black pigs farmed here are cross-bred from European wild boar to get as close as possible to the original stock.

MILDENHALL, AN ATTRACTIVE SUFFOLK MARKET TOWN

The lake at West Stow is well stocked with fish, and is usually encircled with the green umbrellas of patient fishermen and boys. Nearby the Lackford gravel pits have been transformed into a bird-watcher's nature reserve with two hides and abundant waterfowl. The honking of the resident geese flocks can be heard for miles.

The river flows on, through the sandy soil, pine forests, and tangled heaths of Breckland. It passes Icklingham, where in 1974 archaeologists found the site of an early Roman villa. In 1942, on the edge of the fens between West Row and Mildenhall, an even more valuable discovery was unearthed by a farmer's plough. The Mildenhall Treasure, which was declared Treasure Trove and now resides in the British Museum, was a magnificent hoard of Roman silver which also dated back to the fourth century. The treasure consisted of bowls, dishes, platters, goblets and spoons, all richly decorated in naturalistic classical images of maidens and satyrs, of the gods Pan and Bacchus, and a drunken, dancing Hercules.

At Mildenhall the river briefly splits, passing under two gracefully arched wooden footbridges which connect its banks with the little wooded Parkes Island. Mildenhall is another ancient and thriving little market town, and close by is the giant USAF fighter and transport base, which hosts what is arguably the most spectacular annual air show in England. The Red Arrows air display team are among the regular visitors here, splitting the immense Suffolk skies with multi-coloured vapour trails, in intricate daredevil patterns, above thousands of enthralled, upturned faces.

The River Lark rejoins itself and then leaves Mildenhall, broader now, but still placid to continue its journey through the vast open fens to its meeting place with the Great Ouze. And then, as part of that greater river, onward to its final merging with The Wash and the North Sea.

AT FRAMLINGHAM CASTLE, THE MUSKETEERS AND PIKEMEN OF THE ENGLISH CIVIL WAR SOCIETY RE-CREATE THE MUTINY OF 1648

Suffolk castles – strongholds of the Normans

2

2 SUFFOLK CASTLES – STRONGHOLDS OF THE NORMANS

Take the high ground, and hold the high ground, have always been sound military maxims. When prehistoric man first emerged from his caves it probably did not take him long to work out that it was easier to defend a hill than a valley. When the neighbours turned hostile it was always easier to beat them back from a greater height. Rocks would roll downhill, but not up, and it took less energy to throw spears and axes if you used, rather than opposed, the downhill pull of gravity. If there was a natural ring of boulders to hide behind so much the better. You could hurl missiles and then duck down safely when the barrage was returned. Gradually the idea dawned that if there were no such natural defences you could always make some. So the first fortified hilltop camps of the Stone Age came into being. Log palisades were erected to ring the site. Defensive ditches were dug outside the palisades and the earth used to raise the level of the hilltop inside, and so the idea for the first primitive castles was born.

The Romans came and built walled towns, much stronger than the old hill-top forts, and then centuries later, after the fateful Battle of Hastings in 1066, it was the turn of the Normans. To hold his new-won kingdom William The Conqueror gave control of most of the old Saxon manors to his own favoured knights, who soon began building the great stone, battlemented monuments with a square central Keep and massive outer bailey walls, that give us our modern romantic model of a mediaeval castle. Many such castles were built in Suffolk, some such as those at Haughley and Walton have disappeared, but in various stages of ruin a few of them still survive today.

One such favoured knight was Richard FitzGilbert, who was given control of 170 manors in Essex and Suffolk. FitzGilbert built his castle at Clare in a bend of the River Stour which forms the Essex/Suffolk border, using an existing Saxon earthwork, and surmounting it by two bailey walls, both fenced and moated. It had a wooden central tower, which was later replaced with a stone keep, and the curtain wall was later reinforced with four more stone towers. Today only one great stump of the Keep wall remains on top of the great castle mound in the centre of what is now Clare's country park. However, Richard FitzGilbert had changed his family name to de-Clare, and due to the many and varied enterprises of his descendents it is a name that has since gone down in history. Clare College in Cambridge, County Clare in Ireland, the Dukes of Clarence, and even the name claret, synonymous with the fine red wines of Bordeaux, are all derived from the name de-Clare.

Further north in Suffolk all the Saxon lands that had been held by Edric of Laxfield were given to William Malet, another Norman Knight who had fought with The Conqueror at Hastings. Malet was responsible for building the castle at Eye, and is believed to have later died fighting Hereward The Wake, perhaps the last of the Saxon defiants, in the rebel-held marshes of the Fens. The Castle he raised was of typical Norman construction on the only high ground in north Suffolk, with the natural hill elevated by layers of imported soil and surrounded by inner and outer Bailey walls. The town saw full scale sieges in the Middle Ages, the first in 1173, and again when the castle came under attack and was sacked in the Barons War of 1265.

EYE CHURCH
AND GUILDHALL,
OVERLOOKED BY
THE CASTLE WALLS

From the few grey-stone ruins that remain on the castle mound there are now fine bird's-eye views over modern Eye, especially the view of the magnificent, flint-paneled Church of Saint Peter and Saint Paul which towers over its elegant neighbour, the black and white timbered fifteenth century guildhall. The great oval of the town centre, marked out by Church Street, Broad Street and Castle Street, show the outline where once stood the old bailey walls.

There is a village atmosphere to this lovely small town, but a town it definitely is with an imposing town hall to prove it. Standing on an island in the centre of Eye, with traffic flowing by on either side, it is a square and solid-looking building, a no-nonsense sort of building, yet smart and attractive in its red brick with its neat lozenge panels of small black flints. It was designed by Edward Buckton Lamb and opened in 1587 to replace the old Corn Hall, and is now crowned by an elegant clock turret that was given by Charles Tacon to commemorate Queen Victoria's Jubilee.

The Jubilee Clock was designed to keep accurate time, and time here has seen the proud walls of Eye castle crumble and fall as the powers of its mediaeval masters waxed and waned. However, it is still a delightful little town to explore with a heady mixture of architectural styles and materials lining its streets.

The Norman castles were the strongholds which the Barons could hold for or against their King, or from which to sally forth to fight for their King, or against him, or against each other, depending upon their current ambitions and inclinations. The twelfth century saw much of this belligerent scheming, and the galloping to and fro of Knights and men at arms. The central characters in Suffolk were undoubtedly the powerful Bigods who held their castles at Bungay and Framlingham.

William the Conqueror granted 117 Suffolk manors to the first Roger Bigod, and it was Roger's son Hugh who built the first Norman castles on both sites. A tyrannical bully, by all accounts, Hugh not only terrorised the local Saxons, but frequently rebelled against his King, attacking the royalist castles, surrendering, or changing sides, whichever became politically or militarily expedient. Generally he was successful in his rampaging, and it was said in his time that whoever wore the Crown in London, it was the Bigods who effectively ruled Suffolk.

Eventually Hugh Bigod provoked his King too far by supporting the sons of Henry II in an armed revolt. Henry set about containing his troublesome Baron by building his own massive castle at Orford to control the approaches to Framlingham from the sea. With the castles at Norwich, Eye, Thetford and Walton, also in Royalist hands, Hugh Bigod was trapped within a royal cordon. Hugh hired French and Flemish mercenary troops and launched a defiant bid for independence. His ally, the Earl of Leicester, attacked and destroyed Haughley Castle, smoking out the defenders with fire and pushing what was left of the castle into the moat. However, Henry himself marched a royal army upon Framlingham, where Hugh Bigod, the bane of Suffolk at last surrendered.

The castles at Bungay and Framlingham were both dismantled, Bungay only partially before Hugh could buy off Henry for a price. Hugh's successor, the next Roger Bigod, succeeded in reclaiming his father's estates and in rebuilding both castles on their original sites. By this time Henry had been succeeded by Richard the Lionheart who desperately needed money to finance his crusades, which meant that Roger could also redeem Framlingham for another ransom.

THE MIGHTY WALLS OF FRAMLINGHAM CASTLE

The new Framlingham castle, the one which still stands today, was even more massive and formidable than the one before. Roger managed to remain loyal to Richard, but not to the next King, King John. To his credit Roger Bigod was one of the barons who combined to force John to sign the Magna Carta. Again the reigning Bigod and the reigning monarch were at war, and again Framlingham was besieged by the King's army. The castle surrendered. The fortunes of war turned against John, and again history repeated itself. After the dust of the last bloody campaigns had settled, the Bigods still held their castles and their titles of Earl of Norfolk for the next hundred years.

The last Bigod, Roger Bigod the Fourth, refused to go to Gascony to fight for King Edward the First, and finally enough was enough. On Roger's death in 1307 his castles, his estates and his titles were confiscated by the King. The long succession of Bigod thorns in the royal side passed into history.

THE SPLENDID KEEP OF ORFORD CASTLE

Orford and Framlingham together give us an almost complete picture of what the ideal Norman castle would have looked like. At Framlingham it is the massive circle of the outer walls and towers that remain. Each of the thirteen towers had a fighting gallery at the top, and the fields of fire from the towers, and the parapets of the great walls would have mercilessly rained arrows on attackers from any direction. Nothing remains inside Framlingham now, except the grey flint poorhouse that was only rebuilt in 1792. However, at Orford it is the walls that have disappeared, and what remains there is the magnificent stone tower of the keep. Imagine Orford inside the walls of Framlingham and you have the perfect picture.

Both castles overshadow their surroundings. Orford towers over the quiet, natural beauty of the River Alde and the old barge quay that is now visited more regularly by a wide variety of modern pleasure craft. The walls of Framlingham dwarf the small market town of the same name which is worth a visit in its own right.

The centre of Framlingham is the triangular Market Hill where a market has been held since the Thirteenth Century. Lively annual fairs were also held here at Michaelmas and Christmas. The town has three churches, including the Sixteenth Century St. Michael's which holds some of the finest tombs in the county. There are several notable almshouses, an ancient guildhall which is now divided into shops and offices, and on the outskirts the splendid red brick Framlingham College.

In the Seventeenth Century a large number of witch trials took place here, and you can still find the ducking pond where the suspected witches were ducked to see if they lived or drowned. If they lived, of course, it was because they truly were witches in league with the Devil.

Between the College and the Castle, on the north side of the town, is The Mere, which was once a fair-sized lake. In the Twelfth and Thirteenth centuries it could be reached by small ships from the sea, and its waters and water meadows provided the town with plentiful supplies of deer, fish and waterfowl. Today it is managed by the Suffolk Wildlife Trust and its circular walks can still give glimpses of swans and ducks, and the occasional kingfisher or heron.

The invention of canon, the fore-runner to modern artillery, brought about the decline of the mediaeval castle. Their massive walls were no longer impregnable when cannon balls could knock them down. The ruins that remain are now museum pieces, and romantic playgrounds for our imaginations. Although from time-to-time the past can be recreated.

THE WALLS OF BUNGAY CASTLE, DECKED OUT FOR CARNIVAL WEEK

The last day of Bungay's two week festival in July saw medi-aeval banners and pennants flying again to give bright splashes of defiant colour to the ruined walls of Bungay Castle. A pageant of living history was vigorously enacted by the members of the Plantagenet Medieval Society, with archery contests, sword and axe-fighting drills, a graceful dancing interlude of minuetes by the castle ladies, and a rousing finale of challenging combat by the knights at arms. The crash of sword, axe, mace and shield echoing again as the pages of history flashed backwards to the days when Hugh Bigod ruled from his high walled stronghold by the Waveney.

A few weeks later it was the turn of Framlingham Castle to re-enact the crisis in the army during the English civil war. The members of the Fairfax Battalia of the English Civil War Society played the role of the garrison of Framlingham Castle to re-create the year of 1648. Pikemen and musketeers marched to their battle drum, drilled and charged, and finally mutinied. The display, like that of the knights at Bungay, paid great attention to the accuracy of the events portrayed, and to every pains-taking detail of the dress, weapons and lifestyle of the eras they depicted. They were living history lessons, bringing the past vividly alive.

Suffolk's castles are now as obsolete as the stone-age rock throwing that defended the first besieged hilltop, but they and the towns and villages they dominate are still well worth a visit at any time. They are a solid link with the great, and infamous, names and deeds of the past, and a feast for the imagination. And if you are lucky enough to catch one of the living history displays so much the better.

ARCHERS DEMONSTRATE THEIR SKILLS AT BUNGAY CASTLE

SUFFOLK'S GLORIOUS GUILDHALLS

3

3 SUFFOLK'S GLORIOUS GUILDHALLS

Wool was the wealth of Suffolk in the middle ages, and the rich legacy of that golden age is all around us; in the crooked-timbered merchant's houses that grace so many of our towns and villages, in splendid churches that soar into those vast blue skies above our gently rolling landscapes, but most of all in a collection of magnificent mediaeval guildhalls.

LAVENHAM, THE MEDIAEVAL FRONTAGE OF WATER STREET

The crown jewel of all the once-flourishing wool towns is, of course, Lavenham, its splendidly twisting streets of colour-washed, crazy-angled, black and grey-beamed houses, all seemingly suspended in its sunlit nostalgic past. Take away the modern traffic, scatter the surrounding fields with a multitude of sheep, clothe its inhabitants in the wigs, frockcoats and stockings of yesteryear, and it might seem that time has frozen and that Lavenham is truly a living museum.

At its heart, now, as then in its glorious past, stands the Guildhall of the Guild of Corpus Christi, built in 1529, and perhaps the finest of all of Suffolk's surviving guildhalls.

The wool trade thrived in Suffolk through the middle ages, not because of the superior quality of Suffolk wool, but because Suffolk, and East Anglia generally, had the prime advantage of being closer to Europe than any of the other English counties. Major waterways like the Stour, the Deben and the Orwell carried the woolsacks easily to the ports of Harwich, Woodbridge and Ipswich, supplemented by the pack horse convoys of the wealthy merchants that wended the convenient old Roman roads from the wool towns to the coast. London was also within relatively short reach of the Suffolk wool centres, and so Suffolk was ideally placed to serve both the export and the home markets with its surplus wool.

The Dark Ages ended gradually in the eleventh century, with the slow curtailment of the Viking raiders and the restoration of some political order, allowing room for commerce and trade to develop. The textile and clothing markets flourished in the low countries and the Baltic, but much of the land in Flanders was too water-logged and the sheep flocks suffered from foot-rot, and so these markets soon came to depend heavily on English wool. The coming of the Normans, although fiercely resisted by the luckless Saxon King Harold in the battle of Hastings in 1066 (The only date every English schoolchild remembers), at least led to the stability and security that attracted the wealthy foreign buyers from Europe to the growing wool towns of Suffolk and East Anglia.

The guilds which grew in wealth and power with the wool trade were the trades unions of the master craftsmen in an age before industrialisation and the appearance of factories could concentrate productivity under one roof. Individual weavers, spinners, dyers and the rest worked mostly in their own homes, and the guilds were the mediaeval way of forming themselves into brotherhoods to protect their own interests in the regulation of trade, wages, prices and standards. The guilds elected their own warden and aldermen to act in the roles that would now be defined as the chairman and committee members to debate and manage their affairs, and their own inspectors to guarantee that the quality of work and goods was maintained. There was a strong sense of pride in ensuring the highest standard of craftsmanship.

However, the regulation of trade was not their only concern. They were a social force and most crafts made some efforts to see to the welfare of any members and their families who might fall on hard times through injury or old age. There were ceremonial and religious events to be recognised and supported, and each guild had its own livery to be worn when the occasion demanded. The guildsmen in their finery provided a proud and colourful element in every important procession and congregation that brought festive and feasting life to the wool towns.

Undesirable elements were not welcome, and before a craftsman could join a guild he would generally need to be a property owner of some standing. Membership tended to be passed carefully from father to son, although some exceptions were made and a membership might be bought after a long apprenticeship. The smaller guilds would meet in their own homes, or meeting houses, but the larger guilds were able to found the magnificent guildhalls, of which a few survive today.

THE GUILDHALL OF CORPUS CHRISTI AT LAVENHAM

Lavenham, at the height of its prosperity had four guildhalls. Two have disappeared with the passage of time. The Guildhall of Our Lady still survives as part of the Swan Hotel at the bottom end corner of Lady Street. At the top end of Lady Street is, of course, the Market Square, faced by that magnificent, grey-toned, three-storied Guildhall of the Guild of Corpus Christi. Beautifully timbered with overhanging beams at first floor level, and gable windows jutting out of the slanting angles of its red-tiled roof, it has elegant oriel windows, a carved porch doorway, and on one corner post on the junction with Lady Street, a carving that is believed to be of John de Vere, the fifteenth Earl of Oxford, who granted the Guildhall its original charter.

LAVENHAM, THE GUILDHALL OF OUR LADY,
WHICH IS NOW PART OF THE SWAN HOTEL

In the nearby wool town of Hadliegh stands the second show-piece survivor of those prosperous middle ages when wool towns were Suffolk's El Dorados. Set, like Lavenham, on the gentle river Brett, which provided the power to drive its mills and the running water to wash its wool, Hadliegh also generated the wealth to build its own prestigious Guildhall in 1438. The wealthy clothier William de Clopton paid for this brand new Market Hall and rented it to the town at the nominal fee of one red rose per annum. After his death the grateful townspeople continued to pay the token sum, placing the annual red rose on Clopton's tomb in Long Melford Church.

In its hey-day the Hadleigh Guildhall was the centre of commercial life and served as a meeting place for all five of the town's major guilds; Corpus Christi, Our Lady, Trinity and St. John's. Today it is still used for parish functions. It stands in the quiet heart of town, eye-catchingly resplendent in orche-red plaster with black timbers and beams, its central section rising to three stories and topped by red-brick chimneys. Across the old grave-yard of grey, lichen-filigreed headstones it faces St. Mary's church with its slightly-crooked silver spire soaring 135 feet above its fourteenth century tower. Beside the church is the red-brick Deanery tower, built in 1495 to serve as the Deanery Gateway. Here is the heritage centre of Hadleigh, almost out of sight and sound of the by-passing bustle of High Street traffic.

THE GUILDHALL AT HADLEIGH

EYE, THE GUILDHALL

Guildhalls and churches go hand in hand in Suffolk, for in many cases it was the riches from the wool trade that also built the churches. The wool merchants were pious as well as wealthy, and by donating to the churches they guaranteed that the congregations would pray for their souls. In Eye the lovely two-storied black and white guildhall stands beside the overshadowing tower of the Church of Saint Peter and Saint Paul, both of them facing the rising grass mound topped with the few remaining walls of the ancient castle keep. The Eye Guildhall was built in the late sixteenth century and carefully restored in 1875. An original carving of the Archangel Gabriel can still be seen on one of its wooden corner posts.

At Stoke-by-Nayland in the lovely Stour valley there is another fifteenth century Guildhall, again nestling in the comforting shadow of the mighty 120 foot high tower of its church companion. It stands opposite the lychgate so that the guildsmen would only have had to march across the road to reach the west door in the tower. In its glory days there were again four guilds in Stoke, so although the distance was short, their massed processions would have made a fine sight as they crossed from the Guildhall to attend a church service.

All over Suffolk the remaining guildhalls, the wool churches, and the multitude of fine timbered merchant's houses all testify to the wealth and power of the golden age of wool. The Suffolk-pink, thatch-roofed building beside the Post Office in Debenham High Street was once the Guildhall of Holy Trinity, the lovely old Fox and Goose public house in Fressingfield was also once a guildhall.

In addition to the merchants guilds in the towns there were also many church or parish guilds in the rural areas, which were made up of friends and neighbours and usually centred on the parish church. The trade guilds had their social and religious aspects but the salvation of the soul was not an obsession restricted to rich traders and wool merchants. Prayers for the deceased were a vital function of all guilds, and the parish guilds also grew on the legacies of their benefactors. A prime example remains in the Guildhall at Laxfield, dedicated to the Guild of Saint Mary which was established in 1452. The actual Guildhall was built later in the early Sixteenth century after the work, needs and wealth of the Guild had outgrown its church origins.

THE GUILDHALL, WHICH IS NOW THREE SEPARATE DWELLINGS,
AND THE PORCH OF ST. MARY'S CHURCH AT STOKE BY NAYLAND

What survives today is a superb, mainly oak-framed building, with walls of herring-bone patterned red bricks filling the bays between the main posts. The upper floor overhangs the lower in the usual Tudor fashion and today the building houses the Laxfield and District Museum.

There were ups and downs throughout the four centuries that the wool trade remained the dominant part of Suffolk's commercial life. Political interference, swinging taxes and foreign wars all took their toll in disrupting the smooth flow of trade. The guilds themselves were dissolved by Acts of Parliament in the late sixteenth century, falling foul of Protestant reformers because of their close associations with what then came to be seen as mediaeval religion. But finally it was the industrial age, the factory chimney and the factory siren, that signaled and sounded the death knell of the wool trade, and the boom times of the laden packhorse convoys and river barges carrying the white harvest to the coast. The scattered, individual craftsmen working in their own homes could not compete with the concentrated output of the factories. Good grazing pastures, clean-running rivers and a short haul to the coast, were no longer the crucial factors to commercial success. Coal was the New King, and the factories went where there was coal on hand to power them. Suffolk had no coal and suffered an irreversible decline, as the heart of the new industrial age shifted to the Midlands and the north.

The age of the Suffolk wool barons is over. The vast sheep flocks no longer bleat in summer snow-fields on every acre of lush grass. The stout, white-wigged and resplendently frock-coated burghers no longer rule the rural roost. The majestic guildhalls, trade and parish, no longer throb and thrive with the hub-bub of daily prayer, bargaining and business.

But Suffolk's heritage remains preserved in Lavenham, Hadleigh, Stoke and Eye, and almost any other Suffolk town that thrived in the golden age of wool.

Suffolk's Abbeys
– on the way to God

4

4 SUFFOLK'S ABBEYS
– ON THE WAY TO GOD

In the Middle ages the great abbeys of England and the monastic orders that ruled them, were a power in the land to rank with the mightiest of Barons, and even the King. Not until King Henry VIII dared to dissolve them in the Sixteenth Century were they finally toppled into the splendid ruins which are their legacy today. Suffolk has several magnificent reminders of those mediaeval days of ecclesiastical glory, scattered in jewels of wind-scoured flint and rain-bleached stone that still defy the efforts of time and man, and the elements to obliterate them entirely.

THE ABBEYGATE, BURY ST. EDMUNDS MOST FAMOUS LANDMARK, AND NOW THE MAIN ENTRANCE TO THE ABBEY GARDENS AND RUINS

MASSIVE, ERODED FLINT COLUMNS MARK THE SITE OF THE
HIGH ALTAR IN THE ABBEY RUINS AT BURY ST. EDMUNDS

The prime example of the peak period of Suffolk's monastic dominance lies in the still awesome Abbey Ruins in the heart of Bury St. Edmunds. Here the solid square block of the Abbey Gateway with its huge raised portcullis gate still stands almost intact. Nearby is the tall Norman Tower, that now acts as the bell tower for St. James Cathedral, which today stands in a corner of the original site. Inside the Abbey Gardens the ruins are great monoliths of rugged flint. Just inside the Abbeygate is a framed picture of W.K. Hardy's imagined drawing of how the Abbey probably looked just before the Reformation. It shows a mighty church with two sky-piercing towers at least four times the height of the surviving gateway, and probably twice the size of the present cathedral. It must surely have been a gigantic testament to the faith and power of its age.

The first monastery to be established here was built by the Saxon King Sigbercht, a son of the great Raedwald of Sutton Hoo, around the turn of the seventh century. The death and martyrdom of Saint Edmund in 869, and the subsequent internment of his remains at Sigbercht's monastery, turned it into the great mediaeval shrine it eventually became. In 1016 the Danes conquered all of England, and Thorkal the Tall, the Danish Earl who was made master of East Anglia, replaced the secular priests at the shrine of St. Edmundsbury with twenty Benedictine monks. Under the Benedictines the Abbey flourished to its greatest heights, surviving the Norman conquest intact, probably because its Abbot at the time was not only a brilliant administrator, but also a Frenchman.

The Benedictines followed the rule of Saint Benedict of Nursia, who founded the first twelve monasteries at Subiaco near Rome in the 6th Century when he organised his followers into communities. His rule of life, which incorporated communal living, physical labour, and the distribution of food and alms to the poor, became the model for the other monastic orders that followed, and revitalised the whole concept of monastic life in central and western Europe. The order had over 15,000 monks by the end of the fifteenth century, but after the cataclysm of the Reformation less than 5,000 remained.

St. Edmundsbury at its height is said to have contained some 80 Benedictine monks, plus the Abbot, some twenty chaplains and over a hundred retainers and servants. It's privileged position as a centre of pilgrimage made it not only the largest and most wealthy abbey in Suffolk, but also one of the five greatest abbeys in the country. Most of the other religious orders were also represented in Suffolk, but they were all over-shadowed by the Benedictines who had seven other priories, nunneries and religious houses scattered around the county.

Their daily routine, (for those not directly engaged in administration, power politics, and the entertaining of visiting Kings and notables), was one of four to eight hours of prayer and the celebrations of their divine office, seven hours of sleep, and the rest of the time divided between religious study and necessary work, mainly agricultural in the gardens and vineyards.

GRAVESTONES AND RUINED WALLS AT LEISTON ABBEY

St. Edmundsbury's nearest rival, in terms of size and power, was probably Leiston Abbey, built in 1182 by Sir Ranulf de Granville, a local Land-owner and Lord Chief Justice to King Henry the Second. His original abbey was constructed in the Minsmere marshes, close to the Suffolk coast, and some three miles from the site of the present abbey ruins.

Leiston was an abbey of the strict Premonstratensian order, which favoured remote and isolated locations away from the distractions and temptations of towns. However, de Granville's first choice of location proved to be a bit too lonely and windswept, and also liable to frequent flooding. After two hundred years the abbey had to be moved and was actually taken down and re-erected on its present site at Leiston, where its remains today in another spectacular array of colossal flint columns, walls and archways.

ARCHES IN STONE ENDURE AT LEISTON ABBEY

The Premonstratensian Order was founded by Saint Norbet of Premontre in 1119 in northern France. They attached great importance to the singing of the Divine Offices, and their inmates were ordained as priests, unlike the monks of other orders. Their robes were of black and white, distinguishing them from the black robes of the Benedictines, and the grey robes of the

Greyfriars. Although more austere in some ways they did not have their heads shaved and were allowed to wear beards.

Leiston, along with all the other religious sites and orders, was dissolved in 1537, and the community was turned out. The last Abbot was granted a small pension. The once proud church and related buildings fell into ruin and became a farmyard, until they were saved from further decay in the 1920s, when they became acknowledged as worthy of restoration and preservation.

Further up the Suffolk coast is Dunwich Greyfriars, the remains of a Franciscan Friary, its last remaining walls perched near a clifftop overlooking the sea that has swallowed up the original town which it served. Its arched windows still frame distant views of Southwold across the grey, wind-flecked waves.

The Franciscans came to England in the thirteenth century, taking their name from Saint Francis of Assisi, the gentle patron saint of animals. Their creed was different from that of the other religious orders in that they worked and preached in the towns and among the ordinary people, looking outward rather than retreating into seclusion. The Friars took vows of poverty, chastity and obedience. They owned little or nothing, and lived on donations of fish, livestock and vegetables given to them by the local people. Their charitable work made them fair contenders for the title of the first social workers.

The priory and its large church, hospital and dormitories are mostly gone. Much of it was badly damaged in the Great Storm of 1286. The ruins that remain are probably the walls of the dining room or refectory where the friars took their meals. The fourteenth century main gate in the west wall still stands, and from the road outside it frames the site in a noble arch that once saw ceremonial processions passing beneath.

Lavenham Priory, a neat, white-washed Tudor building on Lady Street, opposite the old Guildhall of Our Lady that is now one corner of the Swan Hotel, dates back to the thirteenth century. It was an open hall house which belonged to the Earls Colne Priory in Essex, and was frequently used by travelling Benedictine monks on their way to and from their great abbey at Bury.

LAVENHAM PRIORY, ONCE A 13TH CENTURY OPEN HALL HOUSE,
NOW OFFERS AWARD-WINNING B&B ACCOMMODATION

After the dissolution it became a private house, owned by a succession of wealthy clothiers and clerics, and for some time by the De Vere family, the Earls of Oxford. By the 1960s it had become a derelict dairy farm, but has once again been renovated into a private home offering excellent bed and breakfast holiday breaks. In 1999 it won the AA award for the best guest accommodation in the country.

THE PRIORY
CHURCH AT
CLARE

On the western side of the county, tucked into a loop of the Stour
on the Essex border, lies the small town of Clare, and the thirteenth century Clare Priory, with its church and the fourteenth
century Friars House. It was founded in 1248 by The Order of
Hermit Friars of Saint Augustine of Hippo, who came from
northern France at the invitation of Sir Richard de Clare. The

Friars kept to strict rules of poverty and saw their mission as one of preaching and tending the sick. Following the rule of their spiritual founder the Friars strove to *'Live together in harmony, being of one mind and one heart on the way to God.'*

Like all the other religious houses in the country Clare Priory suffered dissolution at the command of Henry VIII. However, the order survived in Ireland, and from there the Augustinians returned to Clare in 1953, to re-establish the priory as a religious retreat, where lay people and friars share a common life of prayer, work and friendship in their search for God. They offer a warm welcome to any who wish to join them, for a few hours, a few days, or longer.

It is good to see that one small wheel of faith has turned full circle, spiritually as strong as ever, and enduring even more forcefully than those devastated ruins of the once great abbeys. Perhaps Crass King Henry hasn't had the last word after all.

THE UPPER STOUR –
A PAINTER'S PARADISE

5

5 THE UPPER STOUR –
A PAINTER'S PARADISE

The River Stour meanders lazily through a sixty mile long pastoral valley, through Suffolk fields and landscapes, woodlands and trailing willows, and lush green water meadows, where lethargic cattle browse under vast hot skies in the warm summer sunshine. Its beauty and tranquility, and the wonderful light quality, have inspired numerous painters and artists, Gainsborough and Constable are the obvious examples; and as an easy highway to the sea it has also served the needs of mediaeval trade, and caused castles and stately houses and mansions, and magnificent churches, to spring up along its banks.

For walkers the Stour Valley path runs the whole sixty miles from Newmarket to the river's estuary at Cattawade, with many shorter circular walks at the various points of interest along the route. However, all of its main attractions are easily accessible by car.

As you enter Newmarket from the west there is a superb black bronze statue of a rearing stallion in the centre of the large roundabout on the A1304. It is a life size equestrian poem in motion, and on a fine sunny day with a little heat haze you can almost see the the sleek flank muscles ripple and the flared nostrils snorting. It is a fitting landmark for a town that is famous as the headquarters of British racing. There are over 2500 horses in training here, and on any moring, wet or fine, you can see most of them walking, trotting, or flying at full gallop between the twenty miles or more of white fencing that marks out the walkways and the courses.

It was in the 17th Century that King James the First moved his entire court regularly to Newmarket to enjoy the racing. Horse Racing has been the sport of kings, (and queens), ever since, and was the obvious place to establish the Headquarters of the Jockey Club. The town has two major racecourses and is home to some of the country's major thoroughbred studs, including the National Stud where Visitor Tours are available. It is also home to the National Horse Racing Museum for those who wish to know the whole story in fine detail.

THE CLOCK TOWER AT NEWMARKET

The first stretch of the Stour Valley path starts at the Jubilee Clock Tower, heads down Newmarket High Street, and follows a footpath alongside the Cambridge Road. It takes a turn south just before the Rearing Stallion statue and goes up on to the scrub covered rampart of the Devil's Dyke. This ancient Anglo-Saxon earthwork was built during the 6th and 7th Centuries and was probably part of the boundary of the old kingdom of East Anglia. The path continues through Stetchworth and finally meets up with the Stour where it rises at Great Bradley.

The next noteworthy village is Clare, which we have already visited twice to look at the castle and the priory. Clare can trace its history back to Roman times and the Domesday book, but its heyday began after the Battle of Hastings when the Norman knight Richard Fitzgilbert began the building of a massive Norman castle in a loop of the peaceful River Stour.

Fitzgilbert changed his name to de Clare and for more than two centuries the de Clares were one of the most powerful families in England. Then in 1314 the last of the male line was killed at the Battle of Bannockburn. A few generations later the manor had passed through marriage into the hands of the Crown, and the great castle began to fall into disrepair. Today nothing is left except one massive stump of the Keep wall on top of the central mound.

The town of Clare had grown around the castle, and during the middle ages it became prosperous along with the other great wool towns of Hadleigh, Sudbury and Lavenham. Its one-time wealth is still reflected in the splendid tower of its fourteenth century church of St. Peter and St. Paul. Facing the churchyard is the Priest's House built in 1473, its decorative raised white plaster panels, in a style known locally as pargetting, include beautifully intricate flowers, as well as the arms of the de Clares.

In 1865 the railway came to Clare, and the station was built inside the area that had once been surrounded by the inner bailey walls. Time moves on, another phase of history passed, and now the railway line, the huge steam engines, the cranes, the goods-yards and the livestock pens are also gone. Now there is a pleasant picnic area beside the old railway station and its platforms, and the whole site of the once great Norman castle is now a country park, given over to riverside walks and wildlife, and the silent evocation of its past glories.

CAVENDISH, SUFFOLK PINK THATCHED COTTAGES
AND ST. MARY'S CHURCH TOWER

A few miles east along the stour valley is Cavendish, with possibly the most photographed village green in all of England. Its group of three, thatch-roofed, Suffolk pink cottages, with the church tower immediately behind them, have graced innumerable chocolate boxes, calendars, and magazine covers. It is the perfect picture postcard of a Suffolk village, made magical by the warm play of shadows and that incredible Suffolk sunlight.

The church itself is well worth a visit if you can tear yourself away from the main picture. A Saxon church once stood here until it was replaced from round about 1300 by the present square-towered Norman church dedicated to St. Mary. Inside there is a Flemish altar piece carved in alabaster that probably dates back to the 16th Century, and a magnificent brass 15th Century eagle lectern which is believed to be a gift from the first Queen Elizabeth. The large east window admits plenty of light.

Cavendish was also prosperous during the golden days of the wool trade, and its main street is still one of picturesque old houses and inns. There is a tranquil duck pond right beside the gates to the old rectory which was once a Sue Ryder Home, and still houses the Sue Ryder Foundation Headquarters and museum. Pay it a visit to learn more of this remarkable woman who served with the Special Operations Executive during the dark days of World War II, and who has dedicated her life since to helping the many refugees and victims of its awful aftermath.

Continue eastward along the B1092 and you are soon at Long Melford. Suffolk is a county of Olde Worlde, church-shaded villages, all built around peaceful village greens, and Long Melford has one of the largest at 13 acres, where in more romany-friendly ages the gypsies once held regular horse fairs. The mile long main street that gives Long Melford it's name was probably once a Roman road. It crosses a small bridge at the foot of the green where there once was a mill ford, hence the Melford. The street has many attractive pubs and restaurants, including the splendid old Bull where in 1648 a Roundhead once murdered a Cavalier. Today it is better known as Lovejoy country, because many of its fine buildings are now antique shops.

LONG
MELFORD'S
HOLY TRINITY
CHURCH

However, the ancient heart of Long Melford is still that magnificent expanse of green. At the head of the green stands the red
brick Trinity Hospital almshouse, built in 1573, and crowned by
an elegant white cupola in the centre of the roof. Behind it rises
the glorious flint tower of what is claimed as the finest church
in Suffolk, the Holy Trinity Church, built, like so many others,
by the wealth and piety of the wool merchants, all seeking to
make their small contribution to the permanent Glory of God
in the middle ages.

The interior of the church is a joy to explore. It contains the tombs of John Clopton, the founder of the mediaeval church, and Sir William Cordell who was the Speaker in the House of Commons in the time of Mary Tudor. It also has some beautiful church brasses and a wealth of gorgeous stained glass in its many windows. In the Clopton chapel window is the Lily crucifix representing the traditional flower of the Virgin Mary. Many of the stained glass figures represent friends and relatives of the Clopton family, and one portrait of the Duchess of Norfolk is said to have been used later as a model for the Duchess in Alice In Wonderland. Returning to a more spiritual theme is the famous 'Rabbit window', a small roundel which shows three rabbits, each of which has two ears, although they are linked in such a way that there are only three ears altogether. The image is a symbol of the Trinity.

On the eastern side of the green stands Melford Hall, one of two magnificent stately homes not much more than a mile apart. The other is Kentwell Hall, at the end of a long, leafy drive, behind elegant wrought iron gates, just off the main road to the north. Both are sun-mellowed, red-brick, turreted Tudor mansions. Kentwell Hall was the home of the Cloptons, while Melford Hall was re-built by Sir William Cordell, whose tomb we have already seen inside the church.

Melford Hall has tall chimneys and six lofty towers, each capped with a lead cupola, all spearing the rich blue sky. The house itself being partly screened from the road by a high perimeter wall and neatly groomed, velvet green topiary hedges. Behind the house is a pastoral vista of sheep-grazed parkland. Inside is the original paneled banqueting hall, an eighteenth century drawing room and Regency library. The house is owned by the National Trust and is open to the public.

Kentwell, reflected serenely in its encircling moat and the small facing lake, has been described as the epitome of many people's image of an Elizabethan Country House. It has regular weekends when every aspect of sixteenth century life is faithfully recreated, in its kitchens and bakery, state rooms and drawing rooms, its cow byre, woolshed and wheelwrights shop. All the crafts, costumes, music, mannerisms and language of those byegone days come vividly to life again; and the intruding 'Witchcraft!' of a mobile phone or a pointed camera will cause most of the dedicated players to cross themselves quickly and flinch in mock horror.

KENTWELL HALL, REFLECTED IN ITS PLACID LAKE

Continue following the course of the Stour and you will come to Sudbury, where the house in which Thomas Gainsborough was born is now restored and maintained as a museum in his memory, and the statue of one of Suffolk's greatest painters stands complete with brushes and palette in the market square. Gainsborough is best known for his fashionable portraits, but his real love lay in painting the golden cornfields and those light-rich Suffolk landscapes that lay in abundance all around his home town.

GAINSBOROUGH'S STATUE, OVERLOOKING THE MARKET SQUARE IN THE HEART OF SUDBURY

The Stour flows through Sudbury and a walk back along its banks takes you through The Commons, the sweet, wide water meadows where the traditional grazing rights have been held by the people of Sudbury since the Middle Ages. Today the cows still graze placidly and fishermen, just as placid, ply their rods lazily under overhanging willows. As you leave the town you will pass the brilliant white-board Sudbury Mill, now a modern hotel, where the old mill wheel is still preserved in a glass case in the hotel lounge. A short walk back up the river stands another reminder of those eighteenth century days when the Stour was a working river, the lovely Brundon mill, is also restored in all its white-hoist, red-roofed glory, but as private homes.

FISHERMEN LINE THE BANKS OF THE STOUR BESIDE THE
SUDBURY WATER MILL, NOW A FIRST CLASS HOTEL

The Stour was made navigable as far as Sudbury by an Act of Parliament of 1705, and played a significant part in the commercial life of the town and riverside throughout the eighteenth century. Horse drawn barges hauled coal and goods up river to Sudbury, and on the return journeys transported bricks and corn, cloth and silk, to the estuary for shipment to London and other ports by sea. The large flat barges, known as Stour lighters, worked in pairs, with the second vessel acting as steerage for the first. They carried their cargoes up and down the river until the advent of the First World War, and are immortalised in the paintings of John Constable.

Today the River Stour Trust, which has its headquarters at The Old Granary in Sudbury, works hard at restoring the old locks and landing stages and other navigation works along the river, to preserve the heritage and history of those hard but romantic yesterdays.

THE LOWER STOUR –
CONSTABLE COUNTRY

6

6 THE LOWER STOUR
– CONSTABLE COUNTRY

From Sudbury the Stour winds lazily down to Bures, and another link with East Anglia's historical past, for here on Christmas Day in AD 855, a young Saxon prince was crowned King in St. Stephen's Chapel, which is now known as Chapel Barn. The young King Edmund was to become Saint Edmund after he was killed by the invading Danes for refusing to renounce his Christian Faith, and the chapel was consecrated by Archbishop Langton in 1218. It stands about half a mile out of Bures on the Boxford Road.

BURES, A CHARMING SUFFOLK VILLAGE ON THE STOUR

The village is divided by the river, with Bures St. Mary on the Suffolk side, and Bures Hamlet in neighbouring Essex. The Suffolk side has the church which is largely of 14th Century origin, although a previous church is believed to have stood here before Domesday. The superb solid oak north porch also dates from the Fourteenth Century and is beautifully carved.

As is usual in Suffolk there are many fine old buildings in this delightful small village. The church tower looks down on the main road bridge, and just downriver a smart new, green-railed footbridge now links the popular green meadows of the Recreation Ground with the far bank. Here in summer they hold Bures Music Week, when for me the highlight is the sweet sounds of Jazz swinging lazily in the soft evening air by the Stour.

From here the Stour is flowing through Constable country, turning east past Stoke by Nayland, and through the beautiful Dedham vale and more lush water meadows on to Flatford Mill. John Constable was born at East Bergholt, a mellow Suffolk village with quiet by-roads radiating out into the Stour valley and the surrounding Suffolk countryside. His father owned two windmills near the village, and the watermills at Dedham and Flatford, and his life's work glorifies a boyhood spent here among farmlands, gentle hills and cornfields, river scenes of boats and willows, and shady lanes of ash and oak and red-berried hedgerows. It is hard now to imagine how pure the air must have been before the polluting days of the motor car, how clear and brilliant the sunlight, and how fresh and sweet the rich scents of wildflowers and new mown hay. But Constable knew and loved them all. He captured their very essence in all its richness and colour, and in all its pastoral tranquility, with brush and oils on canvas.

Many of the scenes that Constable painted are still here, the pretty villages with a rich heritage of timber framed and pastel painted buildings, thatched cottages, old coaching inns and impressive churches. Delightful Debden, charm-filled Stoke by Nayland and mellow Stratford St. Mary. And of course Flatford, where there still stands his father's watermill, and Willy Lott's cottage, where he painted *The Haywain*, the most famous of all his works, showing a typical Suffolk waggon half way across the ford. There is a copy hanging somewhere on the walls of almost every other pub in Suffolk.

WILLY LOTT'S COTTAGE, WITHOUT THE *HAYWAIN*

The River Stour flows under Flatford Bridge, a hump-backed, rustic wooden footbridge, that in high summer looks as though it must collapse and sink at any moment under the sheer weight of tourists leaning over its creaking handrails to watch the hired rowing boats circling below. Behind the bridge is the 16th Century, thatch-roofed Bridge Cottage, now a tea shop and information centre for the National Trust. The river divides in two as it flows on to the mill, one fork is checked by the lock with its heavy wooden gates, while the other flows round the back of the island to cascade down the mill race into the mill pool.

Go downstream on the Suffolk bank to see Willy Lott's cottage, and let your imagination picture the haywain, and perhaps Constable himself sitting by the reeds to make his first tentative sketches. Go downstream on the Essex bank, just past the lockgates, to see the peaceful view over the mill pool which forms the substance of what was perhaps Constable's second most famous painting. The water-powered mill was built in 1733 and used to grind wheat into flour, and the granary sacks were transported by 'lighters' up and down the Stour.

A PASTORAL SCENE BY THE STOUR

Go back upstream and you can walk the Essex bank towpath back to Dedham, through the water meadows scattered in midsummer with pic-nicking holiday makers and sleepy, sun-warmed cows. Willows shade every cool green bend of the river, and the rowboats filled with amateur sailors drift blissfully by. The pace of life has slowed here, it's yesterday once more, and folk without hurry are just, 'messing about on the river'.

Continue seaward and within a few miles the gentle Stour leaves its sheltered banks of fields and willows and opens out into the wider estuary that flows for another eight miles to join the Orwell and the sea. Here, at the head of the estuary on the Essex side, are the two small ports of Manningtree and Mistley, where once the horse-drawn Stour lighters would transfer their cargoes into sail-driven craft for their deep-water journeys into the wider world. Grain and flour, malt and wool, went outward to London and the continent. Coal came inward from Newcastle, timber from the Baltic. Where now there are mainly pleasure craft and weekend sailors, between mudflats teeming with waterfowl, there was once the busy traffic of the heavy masts and sturdy brown sails of commercial shipping.

Manningtree was established as a town and port in the thirteenth century, and Mistley in the eighteenth, and although on the Essex side of the river they are still a part of the history of the Stour. Both ports thrived in Georgian times and many of their finer buildings date from that period. The Mistley towers, two matching monuments that stand in the churchyard, may look like a rich man's fantastical folly, but provide notable navigational landmarks. They were built by Richard Rigby as part of the church, and as part of his plan to turn Mistley into a fashionable spa resort. Sadly Rigby went bankrupt, the church was later demolished, and the towers and the unusual Swan fountain in the centre of the town, are all that remain of Rigby's dream.

And so the Stour travels on to pass between the Shotley peninsular on the Suffolk side and Harwich, now today's port for the super-sleek, liner-like modern car ferries to the continent. Shotley was the home of *HMS Ganges*, a Royal Navy training establishment. Up until 1905 there was a wooden warship of that name anchored here for training purposes, but then the ship went and a land base was established that continued to train young sailors until the 1970s. Now there is only the tall mast where the boys used to line the spars and rigging on the ceremonial occasions of its famous heyday, and where the button boy stood on the wind-blown mast top with only the grip of his knees to prevent him from being lifted off into space and those spectacular views all around.

Nearby is Ewarton Hall, for many years the official residence of the Captain of *HMS Ganges*. Legend links the site with Henry VIII and the ill-fated Anne Boleyn, claiming that it was here they first met. The romance was doomed, and despite presenting Henry with a daughter (Elizabeth I) Anne failed to give him the son he desired. So she was finally charged with adultery and executed. However, Anne so loved this part of Suffolk that when she knew she was to face the headsman's axe it is said that she asked for her heart to be returned here.

It was off the coast at Shotley that Britain saw its first major naval battle in a victorious encounter with the Danes. King Alfred The Great, better known for absent-mindedly burning the cakes while he made his plans to defeat the vicious marauders plaguing his kingdom, did not stop at raising an army to turn the Viking tide. He also laid the foundations for what was to become the Royal Navy, when he built and maintained a fleet of fast boats to disrupt the supplies and reinforcements being brought to sustain the invading Danish armies.

AT SHOTLEY A MODERN MARINA NOW OVERLOOKS
THE MEETING OF THE ORWELL AND THE STOUR

Alfred defeated the Danes on land and off the coast of Suffolk
he also gave them a thrashing at sea, capturing sixteen Danish
ships and drowning all his prisoners off what then became
known as Bloody Point.

A large marina now occupies the head of the peninsular, filled
with the jingling masts and staywires of private yachts and power-
boats. There are splendid views over the Orwell to the commercial
port of Felixstowe, the biggest on the east coast, with its skyline
of giant cranes and its docksides lined with container ships from
Hamburg and the Baltic, from Taiwan and Tokyo, Panama and
all ports beyond.

Across the Stour the P & O ships in their gleaming blue and white
livery sail in and out of the Port of Harwich, bound to and from
the passenger ports of Europe. A far cry from 1863 when the

Great Eastern Railway began its first steamship services with three paddle steamers, the *Essex, Suffolk,* and *Norfolk,* which plied regularly between Ipswich and Harwich. It was the coming of the railways that brought an end to most of the commercial activity on the river, but the Stour is still a magical thread, stitching the present to the past, rich in warm memories and a long history.

At almost every turn of the river there is something to see, and today it has been returned to the people; the walkers and ramblers, the fishermen, the Sunday sailors, and to the tourists who come every year to visit Constable Country, and the great houses and other attractions that line its sun-kissed waters.

WHITE SAILS IN THE SUNSET 7

7 WHITE SAILS IN THE SUNSET

There was a time when you could stand upon almost any hilltop in Suffolk and count up to a dozen or more windmills on the surrounding skyline. With their great white sails turning slowly against one of our glorious rose-pink Suffolk sunsets, they must have made a majestic sight indeed. In those days they were as important a part of the rural landscape as the Church Tower or the Manor House, for every community had to have the means of grinding their corn into flour. The Miller ranked with the Blacksmith, the Lord and the Priest, as the essential pillars of human society.

The earliest windmills are believed to have been used in ancient Persia around the 7th Century AD, and from there the general idea of windmills, and of water wheels, is believed to have spread eastward as far as China. The first European Windmills appeared in France and England in the 12th Century, and the first Suffolk Windmill is thought to have been built near Bury St. Edmunds in 1191.

By the thirteenth century windmills were a familiar sight all over our county. They spread like great wooden-sailed wild flowers throughout the Middle Ages and by the 19th Century almost 500 windmills were whirling and grinding away.

Water mills were never quite as numerous, although the use of water power in Suffolk goes back a little further, having first been recorded in Roman times. The Domesday survey recorded 178 water mills in Suffolk, and the needs of the cloth industry pushed this number up to its peak of around 200 mills in the 16th Century.

For around six centuries the tall towers and great wooden shuttered sails dominated our skylines, and then with the advent of steam and oil engines the glorious heyday of wind and water power declined. Now the vast majority of the old mills have disappeared for ever, others remain only as a scattering of foundation stones, or old tower stumps used mainly on lonely farms for store sheds. But a few, a precious few, have been beautifully renovated and restored.

Recently Bury St. Edmunds Borough Council launched a leaflet to promote The Miller's Trail, which links the surviving wind and watermills to the north of Bury in a suggested network of walking and cycling tours. Or, if pressed for time, you can do it by car.

The tour begins in Pakenham, where you can see both the beautifully renovated black-tarred, white-sailed, tower mill, and the magnificent white-boarded Water Mill on its little tributary of the River Blackbourne. Pakenham is actually the only parish in England with one of each type of mill still in working order. See them freshly-painted against a blue sky and both of them gleam like new.

The next stop is Bardwell Mill, a tower which has recently had its cap refitted thanks to fund raising and restoration work by the local community. The internal machinery is still intact and it is the great advantage of the tower mill that even when without wind or sails the task of milling can still be carried out with the temporary aid of a steam engine.

The same principle, of course, can also work in reverse. When a tower mill is sail driven, then a transfer of power from the central shaft to an external wheel and fan belt can also power any sort of auxiliary machinery.

THE GRAIN
CHUTE AND
GRINDING
STONES INSIDE
BARDWELL
WINDMILL

Stanton post mill is a change of style. With tower mills like Pakenham and Bardwell it is only the top cap which turns with its sails to face the wind, usually helped by the fantail wheel which keeps the sails into the wind. With a post mill, however, the whole mill turns on a massive central oak post to face the sails into the wind, again aided by a fantail which can be much larger as it turns on wheels at ground level. Stanton, when I saw it, had two of it's great wooden shuttered sails down for maintenance, all part of the endless renovation work that is necessary with all our surviving windmills.

Thelnetham is another black tower mill, fully restored with a brilliantly patriotic red, white and blue fantail. The sails drive two pairs of millstones, and Thelnetham is one of the few remaining mills that still regularly produce and sell flour. Seen framed against the vast blue vault of the sky from the far side of a gently breeze-blown field of golden wheat it is a picture that epitomised the heart and soul of what once was rural Suffolk.

THELNETHAM
WINDMILL, ONE
OF THE FEW
WHICH STILL
PRODUCES FLOUR

The Miller's Trail also points out the fascinating variety of old Suffolk churches that grace the villages along the route. All Saints Church at Hopton is a lovely example, it stands beside the cross-roads in the centre of the village where you turn off for Thelnetham. A church has stood here since the 13th Century, and at one time at least three windmills were probably visible from the upper levels of its handsome tower, although sadly all of these have now disappeared.

All the village churches are worth a closer look as you travel from windmill to windmill, and the excellent map that is part of the Miller's Trail leaflet will help you to find them.

Away from the Miller's Trail the best known Windmill in Suffolk has to be the perfectly preserved post mill at Saxstead Green. A mill is believed to have stood on this site since 1287, although the present mill dates from 1796. Between 1957 and 1960 it was dismantled and completely refurbished, and is now one of the most popular visitor sites in the county.

Another lesser known but perfectly restored gem is the sparkling black and white 18th Century post mill that stands high on its hill above Holton near Halesworth. You can easily miss it as it cannot be seen from the roadside, but climb the hill and find it if you can, you will not be disappointed.

At Thorpness there is another lovely old post mill close beside the famous 'House In The Clouds'. The latter was the village water tower, served by the windmill which acted as a water pump, the water being drawn from the well beneath the mill's roundhouse. The mill ceased pumping in 1940 when the task was taken over by an engine, but that too became redundant in 1963 when the village was connected up to the water mains. Now the post mill is a tourist attraction, and the water tower has been converted into unique holiday accommodation.

SUFFOLK'S FAMOUS
HOUSE IN THE CLOUDS
WAS ONCE A WATER
TOWER, SERVED BY
THORPNESS POST MILL
WHICH ACTED AS ITS
WINDPUMP

One place where you can also see a windpump and a water-mill together is at Stowmarket's celebrated Museum of Rural Life. The Alton Watermill has been re-erected there and the mill machinery is demonstrated regularly using water from the mill pool. Nearby is the Eastbridge windpump, one of four that once stood to drain the Minsmere Level near Leiston in East Suffolk. This one is a smock mill, a third type of mill which is different from the tower mill in that it has an octagonal wooden tower with eight flat sides. The name is said to have derived from the old farmer's smock of the late Seventeenth Century, the smock mill and the smock-clad farmer presenting much the same shape.

WOODBRIDGE
TIDE MILL,
UNIQUE OF ITS
KIND IN SUFFOLK

One final mill that should not be missed is Buttrum's Mill, standing six floors high on the outskirts of Woodbridge. Built in 1836 and named after a long standing family of local millers, it ranks with Pakenham as one of the best preserved tower mills in the county. And while in Woodbridge it would be a crime not to visit the unique white clapboard tide mill that is such a picturesque backdrop to the vibrant little harbour. It still operates at varying times, depending of course upon the ebb and flow of the tides.

Windmills and watermills are all monuments to a past age, to a more peaceful heritage before the superior efficiency of steam, petrol and electricity. However, our modern technology is not free and it is not endless. The oil reserves that drive almost everything we need and depend upon are polluting and limited. It may be time to come full circle, and over the border in Norfolk the writing is in the sky in the form of a set of new, sleek, ultra modern rotor blades, revolving high in the wind above the market town of Swaffham.

The Swaffham Ecotricity Turbine is one of a new generation of direct drive, variable speed wind turbines converting wind power into vital electricity. It was the first in East Anglia, but there are more on the way. As I write the tallest wind turbine in the world is being planned for construction at Ness Point near Lowestoft. Plans are also under way to build Britain's largest offshore windfarm in the North Sea, at Scroby Sands, just two miles east off Great Yarmouth. Thirty Eight of these brand new modern, three-bladed windmills are envisaged, capable of generating enough clean, pollution-free electricity to power over fifty thousand homes.

We may not initially welcome them, because like any new innovation there are some people who find them visually offensive, but they are the windmill of the future, and soon they may be as acceptable a feature of our rural landscape as those beloved old wooden sails of the past.

Time moves on, and many things turn full circle. Perhaps one day our grandchildren will again be able to stand on any Suffolk hilltop, and see a dozen mighty white steel sails revolving against a glorious Suffolk sunset. In the meantime the old fashioned wind and watermills that remain are still worth seeking out, they are a crucial part of our rural heritage.

ALONG THE WAVENEY

8

8 ALONG THE WAVENEY

The Waveney rises secretly in the misty wet marshland of the Redgrave and Lopham Fen Nature Reserve and slowly becomes more of a river than a stream as it flows eastward to divide Suffolk from neighbouring Norfolk. It is initially a shy, gentle river, keeping well out of sight of the main road as it meanders through pastoral fields and lush green valleys. Swans glide on its sun-dappled surface. Cows sleep on its banks. The hum of a dragonfly's wings, or the warble of a blackbird, are often the only sounds, the soft swish of a casting fishing rod the only human intrusion.

History seems never to have touched its upper reaches, until it passes close by Hoxne, where a sidestream curls out to pass under the Goldlbrook Bridge where the hapless young King Edmund is said to have hidden in a desperate attempt to escape his Danish enemies. The attempt failed, Edmund was betrayed and discovered, and promptly became Saint Edmund the Martyr when he was shot full of Danish arrows in an adjoining field, where a simple memorial marks the spot.

The neat, white-boarded water mill at Hoxne is one of only a handful of the Waveney water mills that are still in existence. None of them are now in working order, but from the time of the Doomsday Book up to the middle of the last century there were as many as sixteen water mills on the Suffolk bank, most of them grinding corn and exporting flour along the river. The land was always as rich in wheat and barley as the river was in fish and wildfowl.

THE WAVENEY NEAR HOXNE, A PASTORAL SCENE

The Waveney flows on ignoring and ignored by the rest of history, until it reaches Bungay where it once found itself engulfed in the great swirl of events of the Middle Ages. For it was on the high ground at Bungay that Hugh Bigod built his massive castle on the Waveney in the wake of the Norman Conquest, from where the Bigods dominated and be-devilled much of Suffolk, and England's, troublesome history for the next two hundred years.

The castle is now in ruins, but re-captures some of its old glory at carnival times when its walls are hung with banners and coats of arms, when mediaeval pavilions dot its greensward, and archery contests and mortal combats by knights at arms are re-enacted. Except that today the non-combatants do not have to flee for their lives, instead they sit comfortably on hay bales, licking ice creams and cheering on the fun.

BUNGAY CHURCHES,
RED-BRICK
ST. EDMUNDS AND
THE TALL TOWER OF
ST. MARY'S

The Waveney was made navigable as far inland as Bungay in the seventeenth century, bringing the town back into the mainstream of rural life as an expanding market town and economic centre. The new life breathed by the opening up of the river was a reprieve in the nick of time, for Bungay had been almost totally destroyed in the Great Fire of 1688. During the eighteenth century it was re-built, with many fine new Georgian buildings which give it it's present day character.

Today it is still a thriving little town with plenty of interest in the castle ruins and several fine churches. Central Saint Mary's with its square dominating tower, is where the famous Black Dog of Bungay burst in upon a terrified congregation on one stormy Sunday in 1577. The monster hound killed two of their number and the event was firmly believed to be a visitation from 'Black Shuck', the very Devil himself. Holy Trinity Church with its round Saxon tower, the oldest complete structure in the town, is one of the few buildings to have survived the Great Fire. The splendid red-brick Catholic Church of St. Edmunds is where the martyrdom of Saint Edmund is depicted in sculptural relief.

In the centre of the town is the grey-domed Butter Cross, surmounted by a white lead figure of justice, where once felons were exhibited in a cage to deter other potential wrong-doers. Today it is still the centre of the small Thursday market which has been held here since 1382.

A few miles further downstream is Beccles, another fine market town, dating back to around 960 AD, and Bungay's slightly larger neighbour. Dominating the centre of the town is the great, grey square block of the 14th Century bell tower of St. Michael and All Angels, where the tower stands separate from the church with its magnificently ornate south porch. There are wide greens along the river, and here at busy Beccles Quay, where swans float serenely between the moored yachts and motor boats, the holiday-maker's Waveney begins.

BECCLES, ST. MICHAEL AND ALL ANGELS AND THE TOWN CENTRE

The railways spread their ever widening network of tracks to both Beccles and Bungay in the mid-nineteenth century. It was the beginning of the end of the glorious heydays of the Waveney as a commercial river. The railways, and then the equally remorseless expansion of the roads and motor traffic gradually took the cargoes away from the sailing barges and the wherries.

However, in recent years the Waveney has been re-born again with the advent of the modern leisure industry. From Beccles onward the river is broad and deep, prime cruising water filled with chugging power boats and bright yacht sails of red, white and blue. Under tranquil summer skies every bend of the river, every bridge and vantage point, shows a new sweep of sparkling and foaming wake-ripples, carved up by every type of pleasure craft, both large and small, between lush banks, water meadows and marshes in vivid shades of green.

The river loops north to take the charming little village of Somerleyton and the red and white towers of splendid Somerleyton Hall into it's loose Suffolk embrace. The village is a large, neat green flanked by lovely thatched and timbered cottages, while the hall is a lavish Victorian Christmas cake built in Anglo-Italian style. There are twelve acres of beautiful gardens surrounding the hall, a glory of colours in summer, and the highlight is of course its famous yew hedge maze, an ideal place to lose yourself if you have an hour or two to spare.

THE CHARMING VILLAGE GREEN AT SOMERLEYTON

The main flow of the Waveney continues into Norfolk to link up to Breydon Water, the Norfolk Broads, and a sea exit at Great Yarmouth. However, a shorter sidestream, the Oulton Dyke, leaves the main river a few miles before it passes Somerleyton to dip down into Oulton Broad, a popular venue for yacht-racing and a whole variety of other water sports, and the only Broad in Suffolk. From there it makes for the nearest sea exit at Lowestoft, passing under the bascule bridge across the main road that can be raised to allow small ships to pass to and fro, and out through the harbour to the open sea.

Once the centre of a vast fishing industry Lowestoft is now mainly a seaside resort and a haven for more yachts and pleasure boats. Only a handful of working boats remain, and most of those are engaged not in fishing but in support services to the offshore gas rigs. One survivor of the long gone fishing fleets is the *Lydia Eva*, the world's last steam drifter, spotless now with green painted hull and shiny black funnel, and with all her interior woodwork and brasswork polished and gleaming, but still preserved as closely as possible to the working ship she once was in the 1930s. Today she is a floating museum, and a tour inside her decks tells the whole story of Lowestoft's fishing history.

The Waveney is a ladylike river, generally serene and calm, despite the occasionally stormy moods when she floods her low-lying banks. But from her humble beginnings at Lopham fen to her proud exits into the North Sea she is a lady loved by generations of Suffolk's small boat sailors and fishermen.

LOWESTOFT HARBOUR, PLEASURE BOATS TO THE FORE,
OIL RIG SUPPLY VESSELS IN THE BACKGROUND

Suffolk's glorious
churches

9

9 SUFFOLK'S GLORIOUS CHURCHES

There are around 500 mediaeval churches in Suffolk, some large and splendid, some small and charming, but each one the heart of its own community, and each one unique with its own special setting and characteristics. Some are well known as tourist attractions, while others are perhaps hardly known beyond the circle of their own congregations, but each one is a towered jewel in flint or stone, nurtured by centuries of faith and prayer.

FORNHAM ALL SAINTS – THE HEART OF SUFFOLK, A VILLAGE GREEN,
A THATCHED COTTAGE AND THE VILLAGE CHURCH

A perfect example is St. Mary's in Bury St. Edmunds, one of the oldest parish churches in England, which has stood on the south west corner of the ancient Abbey precinct for 900 years. Many of Suffolk's larger churches have magnificent hammer-beam timber roofs, always a feature to look up for, and the single hammer-beam nave roof of St. Mary's is distinguished by eleven pairs of life size angels that look down benignly from their lofty viewpoint.

As you walk beneath them, between the carved poppy heads on the bench ends of the wooden pews, you approach the high rood screen that is a memorial to the officers of the Suffolk Regiment who have died in action. The screen divides the nave from the chancel, separating the congregation from the choir, and beyond both is the Sanctuary and the Altar, where Holy Communion is given and received. Great stone arches support the roof between the nave and the aisles on either side.

There are chapels on either side of the chancel: on the south side the Lady Chapel, which contains a stained glass memorial window to Mary Tudor, the sister of Henry VIII, who lies buried in the far left corner of the Sanctuary; and on the north side the Suffolk Regimental chapel which contains many of the Regiment's battle flags.

The general floor plan is fairly typical of most large churches, and Saint Mary's seems to be equally richly blessed with almost everything you would normally look for when exploring a mediaeval Suffolk church. On the left as you pass through to the Chancel is a richly carved oak pulpit, and on the left a gleaming gold eagle lectern. There are memorials and tombs, as in many Suffolk churches, and an absolute glory of stained glass abounds.

Almost the whole story of the Bible is told in the high arched windows, the rich imagery portrayed in vibrant, sparkling colours. All those familiar Old Testament characters are here, Noah, Abraham, Joseph, Samson and Gideon, to name but a few. And the New Testament is equally alive in sun-streaming brilliance, from the gentleness of the Nativity, through the poignant sadness of The Last Supper, to the final, heart-rending moments of The Crucifixion.

THE INTERIOR OF ST. MARY'S CHURCH, LOOKING FROM THE NAVE THROUGH TO THE CHANCEL AND THE SANCTUARY

There are beautiful stained glass windows in so many of our churches, all worth seeking out for their wealth of colour and detail, but for the sheer abundance of stained glass St. Mary's is supreme. Look up high on the wall, where the level of the nave drops to the chancel, and there you will find more coloured sunlight pouring through the Martyrdom of Saint Edmund.

Of course, the most well known churches in Suffolk are the great wool churches such as those at Long Melford, Lavenham, Stoke by Nayland and Eye. All of them marked by their great, perpendicular flint towers soaring up a hundred feet and more into our stupendous Suffolk skies.

ST. MARY'S CHURCH, THE NATIVITY IN GLORIOUS STAINED GLASS

The wool churches were built, or luxuriously furnished and expanded, with the wealth of the thriving wool merchants in the Middle ages. The Golden Age of Wool made fortunes for those who controlled it in Suffolk, but this was a pious age when men and women, however rich, were well aware of their own mortality, as well as being secure in their faith in God. So they became patrons of a great surge of church building. No doubt they believed that the higher the church the more chance they would have that their good work would be noticed by God, and as an added security they usually demanded that the congregations they had so benefited would continue to pray for their immortal souls after their death.

HOLY TRINITY AT LONG MELFORD, ONE OF OUR HUGE WOOL CHURCHES

We have already visited the Holy Trinity church at Long Melford on our tour of the Stour valley. Here again there is another wonderful display of stained glass windows, and with its superb overall decoration of knapped flint flushwork Long Melford can claim to be one of the most magnificent churches in Suffolk, and that means in the whole of England. However, there are some serious contenders for the crown. The Church of Saints Peter and Paul at Lavenham is equally splendid, its huge bell tower rising a breath-taking 141 feet about the ancient wool town and the surrounding farmlands.

Here, on the south porch, we have some of the most beautifully carved stonework in Suffolk. Above the porch entrance is a niche containing the figures of Saint Peter and Saint Paul, and on either side of them a range of shields depicting the arms of the de Vere family, the Earls of Oxford. It was John de Vere, the thirteenth Earl, who was Captain General of the army of Henry VII at the Battle of Bosworth in 1485. The crowning of Henry on the battlefield saw the end of the Wars of the Roses, and the beginning of the Tudor dynasty. In celebration John de Vere urged the creation of Lavenham's great church, and the massive but perfectly proportioned south porch was his personal contribution.

At Blythburgh at the head of the tidal estuary stands the great and mainly 15th Century Church of the Holy Trinity, the Cathedral of the Marshes, another perpendicular jewel in Suffolk's crown. Dominating this beautiful stretch of the Suffolk Heritage Coast, it is visible for miles, like some great heavenly stone ship sailing out of the blue sky and white clouds. Awe-inspiring from a distance, it is equally rewarding inside.

In addition to all this glorious profusion of flint towered churches, both large and small, there are some beautiful church spires to be found in Suffolk. The 12th Century Church of St. Mary at Polstead is unique in that it has the only mediaeval stone spire in the county, but there are many later church buildings with graceful needles pointing to the sky.

The Church of the Blessed Virgin Mary at Hadleigh is a perpendicular style main building with a 12th Century tower, topped by a soaring lead covered spire which gleams like burnished silver in the sunlight. The equally splendid tower and spire of St. Mary at Woolpit is a familiar sight to all who travel the A14, and never more impressive than at night when it is floodlit, almost like the high star of Bethlehem in a mellow, yellow glow. The tower and the spire were rebuilt in 1853, replacing the original spire which was destroyed by lightning.

This is one of the greatest parish churches in England, famous since Saxon times for its Shrine of Our Lady and a healing well. Pilgrims came here throughout the Middle Ages. It had to be on the same tour as the huge abbey at Bury St. Edmunds to which it then belonged.

One of the many things worth looking for inside any church are the beautifully carved bench ends that you can find along the aisles. The pews inside St. Mary's are some prime examples, a hand-polished variety of real and legendary animals which survived the Puritan vandalism of the 17th Century because they were seen to be heraldic rather than superstitious.

There are more than forty round tower churches in Suffolk, many of Saxon foundation. The Church of St. Mary at Rickinghall is a prime example. Some of our smaller, older churches have wooden towers, or a roof of thatch. All Saints at Ixworth Thorpe has both, and is a charming, slightly ramshackle reminder of what our early rural churches must have looked like. It has cream plastered walls and a lovely old red brick Tudor porch, and its origins go back for nearly a thousand years.

The majority of our churches have evolved over time, with different ages making changes or adding to the basic structure. In their art and architecture they enshrine much of our history, and each one is a testament to the enduring Christian Faith they have nourished in the heart of every single community over centuries of worship. Tread softly, for these are hallowed places. They are cherished symbols and forceful statements of The Love Of God.

Wherever you wander in Suffolk there will always be a church tower somewhere on the skyline, often on a hill, peeping from behind a group of sheltering oaks, limes or beeches. In almost every village there will be a Church Lane leading off the main road. Follow it and you will find the peace of a quiet church-yard, the recent graves white marble splashed bright with flowers, and the older headstones time-weathered and garnished with moss and lichens and, of course, the church.

ALL SAINTS AT IXWORTH THORPE, WITH ITS
WOODEN BELL TOWER AND THATCHED ROOF

Churches are not difficult to find and are always worth the effort. You can search for specific churches, or just explore the ones you happen to come across. There is always something worthy of note, and you may be pleasantly surprised at what you may discover. The true splendour of a stained glass window can only be fully appreciated from inside a church. And that is a bit like faith itself, you have to enter into it before you can begin to understand it.

ST. MARY'S AT RICKINGHALL, A LOVELY EXAMPLE OF
ONE OF OUR ROUND TOWER SAXON CHURCHES

RINGS OF STILL WATERS

10

10 Rings of still waters

Most of us enjoy the peaceful charm of a water feature in a garden, a trinkling fountain perhaps, water lilies and flashes of goldfish or a few colourful coy carp. There is a universal fascination in the tranquility of a surface of calm water with rich reflections of trailing foliage, floating clouds and sunny skies. The wealthy landowners and merchants of mediaeval times were no exception, except that their idea of a water feature went far beyond a simple pond and rockery. They favoured a fine wide moat to mirror their fine farms and mansions, and all the changing colours of the seasons.

There are in fact over 850 such moated sites in Suffolk, most of them built during the 13th and early 14th Century. They surrounded manorial or monastic sites, parsonages and farms. Full blown castles with stout walls and defences needed a license to crenellate, which could only be granted by the King, so for lesser persons without the political clout and favour of the great Barons, Dukes and Earls, a deep and handsome moat was the highest status symbol to which they could aspire. A moat was 'God's Mirror', reflecting the splendid home, the wealth and position, of the man who owned it.

After the castles these magnificent moated properties are the best reflection we have of the way life was lived in mediaeval times, and to promote this historic theme the East of England Development Agency and Suffolk County Council have set up a project called Friars and Flyers. The aim of the project is to draw attention to the heart of rural Suffolk. The Flyer's side of it is the focus on Suffolk's wartime airfields, but that's a separate story. The Friars aspect covers friaries, priories and abbeys, and includes many of the mediaeval moats.

MAGNIFICENT TANNINGTON HALL, WHICH HAS BEEN DESCRIBED AS
'GEORGIANISED', BUT WITH HUGE ELIZABETHAN CHIMNEYS

To highlight the promotion, Heritage Promotions Officer Susan Brooks organised a Mediaeval Moats by Horse and Carriage tour, and I was fortunate enough to be invited. The tour started from magnificent Tannington Hall, which most likely originated in mediaeval times as a substantial freehold farm. Today it is 'Georgianised' with tall Elizabeth chimneys, extensive gardens and a pair of black swans drifting gracefully on the placid waters of the moat.

Sadly, Tannington Hall is no longer able to offer horse and carriage rides but at that time it did have an extensive collection of sixty two carriages, most of them original vehicles, and our expedition set off in a grand convoy of five different carriages. Two of them were wagonettes, John, our coachman, explained, with tops that could be lifted off in fine weather. The third was a private omnibus that would have been used to collect and return people from the railway station. The third an Opera Coach, with a raised roof so that passengers could sit inside with their top hats on, and the fifth a shooting brake that would have been used for shooting parties.

We made a fine sight as the five carriages rattled gently through the country lanes, the dominant sound the rhythmic clip-clopping of the splendid white and grey pulling the carriage immediately behind. There had been snowdrops and daffodils in the grounds at Tannington Hall, and now there were yellow flowers just breaking through the green fields of rape, and the first sprinklings of white May blossom on the hedgerows. We passed sleepy orchards, open fields, cottages and houses of pink and yellow.

Our first stop was at Dennington Grange Farm, one of fifteen moats in the Dennington area. This part of Suffolk, Susan explained, had a heavy clay soil, a water retaining feature which made the construction of moats much easier. The modern house is of elegant red brick, but the interior has a wealth of ancient timber beams. Behind the house is a large garden and orchard, surrounded by the moat enclosure. It was an idyllic, restful place, where bed and breakfast is available for anyone wishing to linger in the area.

HORSE-DRAWN CARRIAGES AT GRANGE FARM, DENNINGTON

Our next stop was at Dennington Place, once a moated island where there had been a drawbridge instead of the usual earth causeway to the original mansion. It was then rather a muddy mess as the moat was still being dredged and cleared, but Susan assured us that this was rapidly being put in order, and the site was important because here there was a rich slice of history.

In 1381, at the time of the Peasants Revolt, it was the residence of one William Rouse, who was by all accounts a swindling lawyer with close connections to The Crown, and who held the post of Chief Constable to the Hoxne Hundred. During the upheaval the rebel leader of the local villagers, one James de Bedingfield, assembled a large group of rebels to challenge Rouse, threatening to cut off his head if he did not immediately surrender his control of the group of archers and militia posted on the island.

THE QUIET LANES OF CENTRAL SUFFOLK ARE THE IDEAL
PLACE TO ENJOY A HORSE AND CARRIAGE RIDE

Rouse decided to keep his head and body all in one piece and surrendered, in effect giving the rebels control of the local police force, and a step forward in their aim of trying to create a more democratic form of local and national government. All this was three centuries before the Civil War.

'So here we are,' Susan ended with a note of pride, 'standing in the middle of rural Suffolk, at the true seat of local democracy. It all started here!'

We climbed back into the carriages and rattled on into Framlingham, turning heads and slowing traffic as we made our stately progress through the town and up to the Castle. Thanks to the recent rains Framlingham Mere, once described as the Great Lake beneath the Castle, was again an impressive sight beneath the massive grey stone walls.

Located within the castle is the new Lanman Museum, the museum of moats, which explains the importance and locations of the major mediaeval moats in Suffolk. There was time to visit there, and then to walk the walls, before the ride back to Tannington Hall. There a delicious cream tea was laid in the lovely old dining room with it's low beamed ceiling and red brick fireplace.

There is another cluster of moated properties around the Elmhams, a group of close little villages just to the South West of Bungay, and a tour of these made another superb day out. My first stop was St. Peter's Hall, magnificent in its isolation and set back from the road. It's now a brewery, with a restaurant, and another pair of lordly black swans drifting with the mallard on the surrounding waters.

Following my guide leaflet I next found St. Michael's Green. Once it had been fully enclosed by a large ditch or moat, dug by local commoners to prevent their grazing animals from straying. Some parts of the green ditches still remain, but the most photogenic aspect was the little mediaeval gem of St. Michael's church, with its red-tiled roofs and square Norman tower, on the northern end of the green.

Rumburgh Church, further to the south, was once part of a small monastery, the Priory of St. Michael and St. Felix, which was established just before the Norman Conquest. The top of the stubby west tower is weather-boarded with a red tiled pitched roof, and the old church and the adjoining Abbey Farm are still encircled by the ancient moat. It is another picturesque little gem in a very tranquil setting.

However, perhaps the real find in this peaceful corner of Suffolk was South Elmham Hall. For a stranger it was not easy to locate, until a friendly local lady told me that the signs for FARM WALKS, were actually directions to the hall, but it was well worth the effort.

SOUTH ELMHAM HALL, WHERE THE BISHOPS OF NORWICH
ONCE HELD COURT AND ENTERTAINED

The moated hall, now a farmhouse, was once a residence for the hunting Bishops of Norwich in the heart of a deer park. It was grand enough to entertain royalty, for in 1326 King Edward the Second stayed here on his way to Norwich. It now has a modern visitor centre and offers a variety of farm and wildlife walks, most of them leading to the enigmatic Old Minister Ruins which stand in the shaded isolation of a small wood nearby. The ruins were presumably an ancient chapel, possibly built on an earlier earthwork of Roman origin, but it offers more questions than answers, its secrets shrouded in mediaeval history.

On my way back to Bury St. Edmunds there was time for one last stop, at Rishangles Lodge at Thorndon just south of Eye. Here the mediaeval dukes of Suffolk came to hunt in yet another deer park. It was late afternoon and the light was perfect to reflect the white-shuttered lodge in the calm still waters of my last moat of the day.

In central Suffolk stands Helmingham Hall, a beautiful moated manor house, with magnificent walled flower gardens, walks, shrubs, roses and herbaceous borders which make it one of the key private home attractions in Suffolk. It stands in 400 acres of lush green parkland where herds of both red and fallow deer roam among mighty oak trees, many of them planted over 900 years before.

The Hall was built between 1480 and 1510 and many of its high brick chimneys are partially original. It is a splendid picture of rich red brick walls and gables with wide white windows and doors, all reflected back in the serene waters of the 60 foot wide encircling moat.

Here there are still two drawbridges spanning the moat which have been pulled up every night since the year 1510. It was a precaution that was perhaps necessary during the more turbulent periods in British History, especially during the Civil War when the house was one of the headquarters of a Royalist secret society called The Sealed Knot. They were eventually successful in bringing King Charles II to the throne.

Another initiative which highlights the visitor-allure of Suffolk's rich old country houses is the Suffolk Coast and Countryside *Invitation To View* which can be booked through most central and coastal Tourist Information Centres. Through this scheme country houses and other sites which are not always open to visitors, can be visited by pre-booked tour groups. They include four more deep-moated jewels: Bedfield Hall, which is a Twelfth Century moated site with a white manor house from the Fifteenth Century, Columbine Hall, another moated white manor house with massive timber framing and an overhanging upper story which was built around 1390, the traditional red-brick Elizabethan Playford Hall built around 1560, and Otley Hall, an enchanting mediaeval assemblage of high-reaching red-brick chimneys and roof angles.

All of them were family homes with their own fascinating links to history. In the case of Otley Hall it is through the Gosnold family for whom this was their ancestral home for more than 250 years. In 1602 Bartholomew Gosnold captained the *Concord*, on one of the first voyages to the New World where he discovered Cape Cod. He named Martha's Vineyard there after his infant daughter. Later, he captained the *God Speed*, one of the three ships with which he founded Jamestown and began the colonisation of Virginia , the first English-speaking settlement on the new continent of America. In fact it has been said that the foundations of what was to become the greatest superpower on the planet, were laid at the Suffolk fireside at Otley Hall, where both voyages were planned.

I have not yet seen every moated site in Suffolk, there are so many of them, but I have seen enough to get a general picture of Mediaeval Suffolk through those gracious old halls and homes. I can imagine the simple splendour of life in those great, moated manor houses, the hunting parties of Dukes and Bishops riding through their deer parks with dogs and falcons, the commoners grazing their geese and cattle on the common greens, and the desperate days of the Peasants Revolt. They, and all the other insights into Suffolk and British history, can be glimpsed just briefly in God's Mirrors, those peaceful rings of bright, still waters.

DRIFTING DOWN THE DEBEN 11

11 DRIFTING DOWN THE DEBEN

The delightful little village of Debenham in the very heart of Suffolk takes its name from the river, for it is here that the infant streams meet and merge to take their first winding turns to seek out the sea. It is an old village, going back to Domesday and beyond. Almost every other building along its charming, semi-mediaeval High Street seems to date back to the 15th or 16th Centuries. The oldest house, a black and white timbered gem at the head of the small village green goes back to the early 14th, or possibly even the 13th Century. Parts of the solid Saxon tower of the church of St. Mary Magdalene go back even further to the 12th Century.

DEBENHAM'S CHARMING SEMI-MEDIAEVAL HIGH STREET

It is a village steeped in Roman and Saxon history. A nearby field is known as Blood Field because here a savage battle was once fought against the invading Danes. Possibly it was the same battle in which the Saxon King Edmund, later to become Saint Edmund The Martyr, was finally defeated. The long, thatched-roof, pink-washed house beside the Post Office was once the 16th Century Guildhall of the Guild of the Holy Trinity; testifying, along with the proud ram that surmounts the village sign, to Debenham's importance during the golden age of the wool trade. The village has even given it's name to a popular chain of fashion stores that have spread nationwide, for the founder of *Debenhams* was born here in Debenham.

From Debenham the little river meanders on, through gentle valley farmlands to loop its way around the even smaller villages of Brandeston and Easton. Both are picturesque little spots in their own right, and there are some lovely, leisurely walks here. I wandered the paths through woodlands and pastures on one bright autumn morning when the blackberries were ripe and sweet on the hedgerows, the hawthorn berries were shiny crimson, and the dawn-fresh scent of bracken filled the air.

A country lane at Brandeston led me down to a ford where the Deben trickled merrily across the path, with a narrow footbridge thoughtfully in place for when the river rose higher. The continuing walk gives some wide Suffolk-sky views back across open fields to the stately chimneys of Brandeston Hall, which is now a part of Framlingham college.

A few miles further downstream the river curls past Easton, looping around the popular Farm Park and passing the white clapboard Leatherington watermill before passing behind the village. There is a marvellous old red brick crinkle crankle wall in the village that once surrounded the whole of Easton Park. The wavy curves were designed to give the wall greater strength while using less bricks than the traditional double brick wall.

Easton also has some unique little circular thatched cottages, the sort of fairy-tale dwellings where Goldilocks might have found the Three Bears, or Hansel and Gretel fell foul of the wicked witch. However, they were originally built as homes for the park estate staff. Easton also has a charming village green, faced on one side by the lovely old White Horse pub, close by the church.

A FAIRY-TALE IMAGE, ONE OF THE CIRCULAR THATCHED COTTAGES AT EASTON

The Deben flows lazily on to Wickham Market, a larger village established in Roman times because there was a good ford here. The village grew on the passing trade, and later came the bridge which put it on the main coach road from Ipswich through to Lowestoft and Yarmouth.

Moving on downstream the river reaches Ufford, another ancient village which can trace its history back to Anglo-Saxon times.

The Suffolk Punch, the sturdy symbol of our county in the horse-drawn age was born here, and is depicted on the village sign. Once, before global warming, the river regularly froze over at Ufford, and the annual Ice Carnival was the big event of the year. The ice was thick enough to support dancing and ice hockey.

Finally our small, meandering river reaches the estuary at Woodbridge, and there it becomes a broad tidal flow on its last fifteen mile surge to the sea. The centre of this lovely old town with its narrow streets and many fine timber-framed buildings is the ancient Market Square, dominated by the Shire Hall built squarely of red brick with elegant Dutch gables. Behind the hall, in the centre of the square, stands an old gothic styled water pump and drinking trough under a spired stone canopy, which was erected in 1876. With a background of cream, powder blue and pastel pink shopfronts it makes one of the most attractive town centres in Suffolk.

BEHIND THE SHIRE HALL AT WOODBRIDGE THIS ELEGANT SPIRED GOTHIC CANOPY SHELTERS THE OLD TOWN WATER PUMP AND DRINKING TROUGH

Since the days of the Vikings, Woodbridge has grown from an Anglo-Saxon fortress into a thriving port and ship building centre, and then gradually declined again as the navigable reaches of the upper Deben slowly silted up. Now it has revived again as one of Suffolk's top tourist attractions and in the summer months is thronged with visitors. The great ship-building and ship-owning days are gone, but the picturesque little harbour still brings in the modern day sailors in their yachts and pleasure craft.

In fact, Woodbridge has everything a small town needs to put it firmly on the holiday route map. On the edge of the town stands Buttram's Mill, a magnificent six-storey, red-brick tower mill with white sails and fan wheel. While in the heart of the harbour is the white clapboard tide mill which must surely be one of the best known images of Suffolk. Both mills are fully restored and can sometimes be seen working.

THE HALF-SIZE REPLICA OF THE SUTTON HOO
LONGSHIP PULLS PAST THE TIDE MILL

However, the top heritage site here must surely be Sutton Hoo, where in 1939 a local archaeologist discovered the burial ship of an ancient Anglo Saxon warrior king. He is thought to have been Raedwald, King of all East Anglia, who died in about 625AD. A great hoard of gold, bronze and silver was placed with him in his full sized wooden burial ship, which was then covered by a massive earth barrow.

Only recently the National Trust has opened a brand new exhibition hall to display these discoveries, and to tell the story of how our Viking ancestors lived, and fought, and died.

At the annual Woodbridge Regatta one of the event highlights was the appearance of a half-sized replica of the Sutton Hoo longship, rowed by a crew of eight sturdy Vikings. Sliding out from the Sutton Hoo shore the ship was pulled past the magnificent backdrop of the tide mill and the Thames Sailing barge *Thalatta*, which had been moored for the weekend at Ferry Quay. Gracefully she turned down the river, the square white sail picking a course through the packed ranks of sleek hulls, and massed ranks of masts piercing a blue sky splashed with multi-coloured flags and bunting. The combined oar and sail power gave her a nice turn of speed as she passed under the fascinated eyes of thousands of holiday-makers lining the river walk in scorching sunshine.

At 44 feet in length she had been built to ascertain the structure and performance of the ancient Anglo-Saxon vessels, and now the National Trust plans to build a full size replica to stand beside their new Visitor's Centre. At its full 90 feet from prow to stern the original is believed to have been capable of carrying a raiding force of up to a hundred sword and axe wielding warriors.

THE THAMES SAILING BARGE THALATTA, ONE OF THE
MAIN ATTRACTIONS AT THE WOODBRIDGE REGATTA

We are now into the tidal river, winding between gull-haunted
creeks and marshes on its last broad flow to the sea. Many of
the old villages on the river bank still have the remains of 18th
and early 19th Century barge quays, and memories of the days
when vessels like the Thalatta would have shipped cargoes of
wheat and other farm produce round the coast to the major
towns and cities.

Ramsholt and Waldringfield are the two best known, but now
the Viking pirates, the mediaeval warships, and the majority of
the old sailing barges are all gone. Instead, like Woodbridge, they
have revived as busy sailing centres, their waters thronged with
visiting yachts, sailing dinghies and sleek white cruisers. The great
rust red, triangular working sails, have given way to sails of
pristine white, sleek and swift as a swan's wing, or occasionally
multi-coloured in vivid crimson, green, yellow and orange. The

modern river traffic is perhaps as busy as ever, but it is almost all devoted to pleasure, fun and relaxation.

Near the river mouth is King's Fleet, a deep creek which once sheltered the warships of England's kings. Here Edward III gathered the forty ships of his Expeditionary Force when he set sail to claim the French Crown in 1346. It was the beginning of what was to become the Hundred Years War, and Edward was only the first of five English kings who were to engage in the long and bitter struggle to try and win control of France.

The vast, mediaeval harbour at the river mouth has all but vanished now, but at Felixstowe Ferry there is still a charming time warp of fishing boats, and a ramshackle collection of old watercraft and houseboats moored in the creeks or hauled up on the mudflats. Piles of old nets and lobster pots can still be seen by the old boatsheds on the shingle beach.

The ferry still runs here to Bawdsey on the far side. In 1886 Bawdsey Manor was built on the clifftop, standing in 150 acres of land above the cold North Sea. Looking across the rivermouth it was in sight of one of the forty-foot high, red-brick, circular Martello Gun Towers which still stands above the shingle beach. The tower was built in Napoleonic times to protect the old harbour from the possibility of French invasion.

However, in the dark days of World War II Bawdsey Manor was occupied by the Air Ministry and here the top secret research work was accomplished which resulted in the invention of radar. Thanks to this invaluable work the fighter pilots of the RAF were able to hold off the vastly superior numbers of the German Luftwaffe, and so win the Battle of Britain. In addition to all its charm, heritage and beauty, the range of activities along the banks of the Deben almost certainly helped us to win the Second World War.

HERITAGE IPSWICH

12

12 Heritage Ipswich

Ipswich is one of Suffolk's oldest towns, founded around 600AD and probably one of the first to be built by the Anglo-Saxons as they flooded into East Anglia after the departure of the Romans. They came up the Orwell of course, and through two hundred years through the 9th to 11th Centuries the town suffered Viking invasions from the same direct route from the sea. Then around 1200AD things settled down and King John granted the town its first charter confirming the townspeople's rights to their own laws and to administer their own affairs.

A dozen magnificent churches stand witness to the mediaeval prosperity that followed, some of them dating as far back as the 14th Century. From these, right down to the futuristic black glass walls of the ultra-modern Willis Corroon office block, the architectural heritage of Ipswich spans some seven glorious centuries. A two and a half to three hour walk around the town centre can take in most of the highlights and is well worth the effort. There is usually one weekend in September when many of these historic buildings will be open to the public. It's all part of the Heritage Open Days which are annually held throughout Suffolk.

A good place to start in the centre of Ipswich is the Tower Ramparts bus station. Walk over to the north eastern corner and from here you can see the classic Doric columns of the Bethesda Chapel on the corner of Fonnereau Road and St. Margaret's Plain. Looking almost like a Greek temple with those four splendid columns supporting its massive triangular gable, the Bethesda Chapel is actually one of the more modern of the Ipswich architectural jewels. It was opened in 1913.

Go down Northgate Street immediately opposite the Chapel and within a few yards you will come to the red brick archway of the ancient Pykenham Gatehouse. It's on your right opposite the entrance to the Library. It was built about 1471 as the entrance to the residence of William Pykenham, who was then Archdeacon of Suffolk. Through the gateway the site of Pykenham's House is now occupied by the Ipswich and Suffolk Club, a range of lovely old 16th and 17th century timber-framed buildings that is best viewed from the other side, from Tower Street.

THE OLD POST OFFICE

Carry on down Northgate Street and turn right into Tavern Street, the heart of Ipswich with many more fine old mediaeval timbered buildings. As you turn the corner you pass the Great White Horse Hotel, where Charles Dickens stayed and set some of the adventures of the portly Pickwick. Half way down on the right is the Ipswich Institute and Library, founded in 1914 as a

Mechanic's Institute. Then on your left is the old Victorian Post Office with its ornate frontage and life sized statues above its columned entrance, and then the street opens out into Cornhill and the Town Hall.

IPSWICH TOWN HALL

The Town Hall with its dome and clock tower and the French pavilion roof over the raised centre is a fine example of High Victorian civic architecture, and was opened in 1868. However, the

Town Hall is perhaps now best remembered for that fantastic reception in the year 1978 when Ipswich Town brought home the F.A. Cup. Those tumultuous crowd scenes with the triumphant team displaying the cup from the balcony have surely eclipsed anything else ever witnessed during it's 140 year history.

Go down Princes Street and turn back along the Buttermarket and you will come to the Ancient House with its overhanging upper floor and oriel windows, plus some of the most magnificently detailed pargetting in Suffolk. The inner core of the building is 15th Century, although the glorious exterior dates from the 1670s. The reliefs in white plaster include Neptune, a pelican, a shepherd and shepherdess, and the glorious gold, red and blue coat of arms of Charles II.

A few steps up Dial Lane is the fifteenth century Church of St. Lawrence with its splendid perpendicular tower of black flint. A few steps down St. Stephen's Lane opposite is St. Stephen's Church, also dating back to the 15th and 16th Centuries, and now serving as the Tourist Information Centre.

Carry on down St. Stephen's Lane and turn left along Dog's Head Street and Tacket Street, and on your left you will pass the splendid Gothic style Christ Church, built in 1857 as a United Reformed Baptist Congregational Church. Beside it is the lovely red brick Roman Catholic Church of St. Pancras standing behind Christ crucified on a high wooden cross.

Turn right when you reach Fore Street and head down toward the docks. A short detour left will bring you to The Foyer for Ipswich. It was originally part of Ransome's lawn mower works but its conversion into young people's accommodation in 1997 won it the Ipswich Society's top award.

Immediately opposite is the 'Sailor's Church' of St. Clement, another of those ancient churches built mainly in the 14th and early 15th Centuries. Again, of dark knapped flint with a square-built tower, it stands in its quiet churchyard as an oasis of peace and calm between the surrounding busy streets.

Continue down to the docks and the Old Customs House on Common Quay. Built in 1844 of red brick and white stone it has magnificent balustraded external stairways leading up to the first floor pillared portico topped by a dramatic triangular gable. Here you are facing the ancient Port of Ipswich where war galleys were once built for England's kings, where the wool trade once fuelled much of the town's mediaeval maritime prosperity, and from where galleons once set sail with cargoes of hopeful immigrants for the New World of the Americas.

In the last years of the 20th Century you could still see old four masted sailing ships here, moored among a vast flotilla of bunting-strung smaller craft at the annual Ipswich Maritime Festival. However, the old port has now been splendidly renovated with the new Ipswich Haven Marina, which opened in July 2000, providing 180 new berths for visiting and permanent vessels. There are modern luxury shoreside facilities and apartments, all brand, spanking new, but sadly no more spectacular maritime festivals.

The impressive building to the right of the Custom House, which is partly a modern glass office block grafted on to old red brick warehouse walls, was the former Home Warehouse built around 1880. Now it is Contship's HQ. A little further east on Common Quay are Issac Lord's warehouses, which date from the 15th Century and are the only surviving elements of Ipswich's mediaeval port, together with later buildings they form a complex of national importance to illustrate how the early merchants lived and conducted their business.

THE ANCIENT HOUSE IN THE BUTTERMARKET

THE OLD CUSTOM HOUSE AND CONTSHIP HQ

Heading west along College Street you will pass two more ancient churches, first St. Mary's at The Quay, and then the larger Church of St. Peter, dating back again to the 14th Century, and believed to be on the site of the first ever church in Ipswich. Close by St. Peters is the striking red brick arch of Lord Wolsey's Gate, all that remains of the half-built college which the great Cardinal never completed, due to his fall from power in 1530.

Start heading north again up St. Peter's Street towards the town centre. On your right you will pass Silent Street with another collection of ancient timbered buildings, or you can detour round by the quiet little church of St. Nicholas in another sheltered haven of green. Either way you should now be aiming for those distinctive black glass walls of the Willis Corroon office block.

ANCIENT HOUSES ON THE CORNER OF SILENT STREET

SOARING ESCALATORS INSIDE THE WILLIS CORROON OFFICES

This multi award winning building is unique in that it is built to the shape of the site on which it is erected. It was opened in 1975 and in 1991 became the first building of modern design to receive a Grade 1 listing. Each of its three floors covers approximately one and a half acres, linked by a series of splendid internal escalators. The building houses some 1200 clerical and support staff, and those gleaming glass walls contain 890 3m x 2m panes, plus a further 180 panes around the rooftop restaurant areas.

If you haven't already passed it then don't miss the Unitarian Meeting House just a hundred yards or so up Friars Street. Built in 1699 it contains the original pews, a magnificent pulpit, and Dutch 17th Century candelabra. One of the entrance doors still has a spyhole dating from the days when visits from opponents to their nonconformist form of worship were definitely not welcome.

From here it is a short walk back to the Cornhill and through Lloyd's avenue to complete the town centre circuit at the bus station. However, if you still have the energy you are only a few minutes walk from Christchurch Park with its beautiful Tudor mansion. Perhaps the most beautiful of the town's parks, Christchurch covers sixty-five green acres of avenues, flowerbeds and open fields, in Spring much of it is vibrant with golden daffodils.

The mansion was built on the site of the old Augustinian Priory which was suppressed in 1536. The priory estates were seized by the Crown, and then sold to a wealthy London merchant who built the elegant two-winged brick mansion with its classical Greek columns framing the main entrance and its high Dutch gables.

For four hundred years it was a rich family home, but now it is a museum and art gallery. It houses beautiful collections of porcelain and glassware, and comprehensive displays of works by Suffolk artists from the 17th Century to the present day. They include works by Alfred Munnings, Thomas Gainsborough and John Constable.

After a three hour stroll around the heritage heart of ancient Ipswich, it is pleasant to wind down the day in the art gallery, and to simply soak up the captured charm of the surrounding countryside on canvas painted by the acknowledged masters.

BRIDGING THE GAP

13

13 BRIDGING THE GAP

There is something romantic about bridges, as crossing points for trade and commerce, as meeting places and often as the original camp sites where villages, towns and even cities were first settled. If bridges could talk they would have many stories to tell, of intrigue and adventure and travellers tales, and Suffolk has its fair share of mediaeval and modern gems.

THE MEDIAEVAL PACKHORSE BRIDGE AT MOULTON

In the tiny village of Moulton, not far from Newmarket, there stands a rare hump-backed packhorse bridge that dates from the 15th Century. Built from flint with four brick-lined arches it is just wide enough for a laden packhorse or possibly a very narrow cart to squeeze through. It carried the old road from Cambridge to Bury St. Edmunds over the River Kennet.

Seen first from Bridge Street, looking past a traditional pink-washed, thatch-roofed Suffolk cottage, the bridge rears up in a narrow stone hump beside a mainly dry ford that now carries only the occasional car or tractor.

The 20th Century has passed it by (everything now goes down the A14), but before the age of motor cars and railways, or even the stagecoach, and when the Kennet probably flowed much deeper and swifter than the gentle trickle of today, the Moulton packhorse bridge saw regular traffic. Then its narrow stone walls would have been a tight, single file bottleneck, and an ideal ambush point for highwaymen and thieves. The slow and heavily laden horses probably travelled in convoys for their own protection, their riders keeping an alert eye open for the first sign of trouble, with a ready grip on a defensive whip or cudgel, or the hilt of a half drawn sword.

At Hoxne in the Waveny Valley there is another bridge with historic connections. One of the flint pillars of Goldbrook Bridge informs us that this modern reconstruction, using timber rails to copy the original while a concrete road carries today's traffic, was built in 1875. In Suffolk it is difficult to travel far without encountering some aspect of the story of Saint Edmund, and the legend says that the original wooden bridge which stood on this spot in 870 AD was where the ill-fated King attempted to hide from the pursuing Danes.

GOLDBROOK BRIDGE AT HOXNE, WHERE ST. EDMUND
IS SAID TO HAVE BEEN CAPTURED BY THE DANES

As he crouched under the bridge, harried and exhausted after being defeated in a series of bloody battles with the invaders, he was cruelly betrayed by a passing bridal party. The glitter of his golden spurs reflected in the water below gave him away. He was captured by his enemies and slain when he refused to renounce his Christian faith. He was tied to a tree and shot through with arrows, where a simple stone obelisk now marks the spot in a nearby cornfield.

Beside the bridge there is now a striking black flint and red brick community hall, topped by the figure of St. Edmund and below him a white roundel in the gable wall depicting his moment of discovery by the Danes. The martyrdom of Edmund made him a saint but not before he had laid a less than saintly curse on the bridge where he was betrayed, so that even now, it is said, no bride will risk the ill-luck of crossing Goldbrook Bridge on her wedding day.

Another of Suffolk's historic bridges is the solidly buttressed twin arch Abbot's Bridge in Bury St. Edmunds. Originally constructed in the 13th Century, it formed part of the great flint boundary wall that encircled the abbey lands and vineyards, and the towering Abbey shrine of St. Edmund.

THE COMMUNITY CENTRE AT HOXNE, WHERE THE STATUE OF ST. EDMUND STANDS OVER A ROUNDEL DEPICTING HIS ATTEMPT TO HIDE UNDER THE NEARBY BRIDGE

It was once adjoined by the east gate to the town, which guarded the ford and footbridge over the River Lark. Crumbled slightly by the wear of time it still spans the placid river, now protecting only the ruins of what was once one of the greatest religious centres of mediaeval England. Swans and mallards float beneath its arches, drifting as in a timeless dream through sunlight and shadow. Perhaps they were there in the Abbey's heyday of pomp and glory, and perhaps they will be there still when the ruined stones that remain are only dust to be blown away in the breeze.

THE ABBEYGATE BRIDGE IN BURY ST. EDMUNDS

A central Suffolk village gem of thatch roofs and pink and pastel houses is the setting for what is said to be one of the most beautiful bridges in the county, the mellow red-brick arches of Chelsworth Bridge spanning a peaceful, lushly shaded stretch of the River Brett. There are no dramatic historical links here, just a near perfect scene of Suffolk tranquility. Golden daffodils sprinkle the riverbank in Spring, and flower tubs and hanging baskets give the village houses vivid splashes of added colour in the hot, idyllic summers.

While looking at Chelsworth you are not far from Kersey, and although there is not quite a river here and no bridge, the centre of Kersey village must be the most photographed water crossing in the county. The lovely old main street is hap-hazardly aligned with thatched and half-timbered cottages, and is typical of all those time-mellowed little villages that are so picturesque and plentiful in Suffolk. However, what sets it apart from all the rest is the Kersey Splash, the ford that is often flooded at the bottom of the hill.

SWANS PREEN THEMSELVES BESIDE THE ORWELL BRIDGE

Here we are still in the valley of the River Brett, and the Splash is just a side stream, where ducks paddle and cars are forced to slow and make ripples. The square flint tower of the 14th Century village church stands high on the hill that dominates the village, and is visible from the surrounding countryside with almost every twist and turn of the narrow roads and lanes that converge here. There was once a priory on the opposite hill, although very little of it now remains.

Like so many villages in the Suffolk heartland this rural jewel found its original prosperity in the mediaeval wool trade, thriving on its weaving of the golden fleece. Like so many of the major river crossings, the little ford at Kersey has seen fortunes wax and wane with the passage of time.

At Kersey you are on the doorstep of Constable County, and in the high holiday season one of the most crowded bridges to be found anywhere is the old wooden bridge at Flatford, where you can leave Suffolk to wander the water meadows and the towpath on the Essex side. Here in the tourist haven of the lovely Stour Valley, only a short stroll from Flatford Mill and Willy Lott's Cottage, rowing boats can be hired for a gentle afternoon drifting beneath the shading branches of the overhanging willows.

Flocks of spectators line the creaking bridge, threatening to sink it beneath the sheer weight of their laughing numbers. They gather to watch the amateur sailors performing erratic circles before finally getting their nautical know-how and heading lazily downstream.

However, not all of Suffolk's bridges are ancient spans over slow-wandering streams. The new Orwell Bridge is a majestic concrete arc spanning the broad river just below the busy port of Ipswich, carrying four thunderously busy lanes of the A14. Soaring with the seagulls high over the river it is almost a mile long and 80 foot wide, dwarfing small pleasure craft and commercial freighters and container ships alike.

The bridge is carried on colossal white pillars, marching across the marshes in double ranks with two mighty full-width single pillars standing in the river itself. The central span they support is more than 600 feet long, the longest single span of pre-stressed concrete in the United Kingdom.

Opened in 1982 the Orwell Bridge is a triumph of modern engineering and took three years to build. Over 100,000 cubic yards of cement were used in its construction. A far cry from the few hundredweight of bricks and flints used in the Moulton pack-horse bridge 500 years ago.

We may be rich in mediaeval and picturesque bridges in Suffolk, but we can also compete with the biggest and best in the modern world.

THE KERSEY SPLASH, NOT QUITE A RIVER, AND NOT EVEN A BRIDGE,
BUT THE MOST PHOTOGRAPHED WATER CROSSING IN SUFFOLK

THE ORWELL
– A SAILOR'S RIVER

14

14 The Orwell – a sailor's river

At a rough guess there are some three thousand yachts and sailing craft using the Orwell, give or take a thousand. With so many visiting yachts and so many resident boats visiting elsewhere, even those who sail on the river are hard put to give any more than a tentative estimate. Who would want to count them anyway, when there is so much more to see and do on Suffolk's busiest waterway?

AT PIN MILL HOUSEBOATS LINE THE SHORE UNDER SHELTERING TREES

The north bank of the river is hard sand and shingle and there are some splendid walks. The Orwell country park lies on both sides of the Orwell Bridge with woodland and shoreside walking. Further downriver is Levington, with its beautiful little brown and white 12th Century church, and the infamous Ship Inn, once the haunt of smugglers. From here you can walk down to the river and circle round to the Suffolk Yacht Harbour, jampacked with boats and tinkling masts.

The south bank is the sheltered but muddy side, but with good walks radiating out from Pin Mill, through the National Trust woodlands toward Shotley, and along hard field paths down to Wolverton and the Royal Harwich Yacht Club.

However, despite its endless attractions to walkers, birdwatchers, artists, photographers and fishermen, the Orwell is still at its heart a sailor's river. Those who do not venture out on to the river come to watch those who do. The river traffic is all part of the fascination: the big ships heading up to the port of Ipswich, the white sails of the yachts and the red sails of the barges, the clutter of small craft, all making up an endlessly watchable kaleidoscope of waterborne activity.

To get to the heart of it all I visited Pin Mill Sailing Club and talked to Club Commodore Jeremy Prosser, and to Tony Ward, who was the Harbour master's Representative at Pin Mill. We sat in the clubhouse overlooking the club verandah and a wide sweep of the river. It was a beautiful, bright, blue-skied December morning and the river was calm and peaceful. The tide was out, uncovering The Hard, the three hundred metre long causeway that points out toward the deep navigation channel, and leaving high and dry the collection of old barges, boat hulks, and the houseboats with their rickety jetties leading up into the sheltering bank and the overhanging trees.

THE POPULAR BUTT AND OYSTER INN AT PIN MILL

Tony's family goes back through at least three generations of watermen at Pin Mill. 'In my father's time there were always barges here,' he explained. 'My father served his time as a shipwright, working on barge maintenance. Before him my Grandfather was the ferryman here. In those days Great Eastern Railways ran paddle steamers up and down the Orwell, and he would ferry passengers out to the steamers and bring passengers ashore. Before the war the shipping couldn't get up to Ipswich, so passengers and cargo would have to be discharged here.

'Now they've deepened and straightened the river. There was an old Roman ford near the Orwell Bridge, but the river is now dredged to nineteen feet at low water all the way up to Ipswich. You can probably get anything up to twelve hundred tons up there now.'

The changes on the river mean that Tony's role as Harbour master's Representative, virtually the eyes and ears of the Port Authority at Pin Mill, has now decreased with modern ship to shore communications. 'Also the river is now under constant video surveillance,' Tony explained. 'They've got a camera near the Orwell Bridge and another near the Suffolk Yacht Harbour, and with those two cameras they can cover virtually the whole length of the river from Ipswich right down to Harwich Harbour. So now they have no need to ring somebody like me to find out what might be happening at Pin Mill.'

Over a year ago he had sold the Sail Loft which had long been the family business. Its now an art gallery and chandlery, but originally it was the old sailmaker's loft. 'Where they could knock you up a complete set of barge sails for thirty quid,' Tony recalled. So now his main occupation is with the leasing of the moorings he holds. All the moorings, which are leased out to the various yards and marinas along the river, have to be at least seventy feet from the navigable channel.

Tony has an obvious fondness for Pin Mill and the river, which are both his home and his life. 'It's a popular place,' he enthused, 'and it is a pretty place. It's developed naturally, where so many marinas are purpose built. Of course it hasn't got all the modern facilities, but Pin Mill is a village that's grown up because you've got fresh water and a landing place, and because its on the sheltered side away from the wind. Its a nice anchorage and its got character and charm. It's old-fashioned but some people still like the old-fashioned ways. Some people don't want everything all modern and easy. Here you may have to put your wellies on and drag your dinghy two hundred yards out on to The Hard before you can launch and get to your boat, but for some that's all part of the enjoyment.'

AN OLD ANCHOR, CHAINS AND RUSTING BARGE HULKS,
ALL PART OF THE SHIPYARD CHARM OF PIN MILL

Pin Mill is still the only place on the river with free public access, which means that anyone can put in any sort of craft and go poodling around in the river. This freedom does bring problems, though, both with the proliferation of abandoned hulks accumulating along the riverbank, and the problems of amateur sailors in boats that are not always seaworthy.

'This brings us to the need for sailing clubs,' Jeremy put in neatly 'because it is through the sailing clubs that most people learn their basic seamanship. The Pin Mill Sailing Club has a good social side with an annual regatta and regular sea shanty nights, but we're well geared to the teaching side too. We hold navigation classes twice a week.

'We are a bit relaxed here,' He added cheerfully. 'We're not a purist racing club, although we do hold some races and events. All club events are sailed under the Royal Yachting Association rules which are based on sound seamanship and safety principles.'

I was surprised to learn that there's actually no legal equivalent or requirement for anything like a boat owner's driving license, or a boat's MOT test. 'But the Royal Yachting Association, which is the national body for sailing, does conduct voluntary tests,' Jeremy assured me. 'So between the sailing clubs and the Association we do maintain very good sailing standards.'

'This is a reasonably safe river,' Jeremy explained. 'There are some banks and shoals but no rocks or headlands, so even if you do run aground you probably won't do much damage. But it is a tidal river and a commercial river, and because the commercial ships have to keep to the deep channel they do have right of way. The old idea of steam giving way to sail no longer applies, because even at sea yachtsmen still have to give way to the commercial ships. We have to treat the commercial routes in the same way as pedestrians crossing the main road, look both ways and make sure that its clear.'

In addition to Pin Mill there are half a dozen purpose built marinas along the Orwell. It is a wide safe river, popular with yachtsmen, and within easy weekend sailing of the Deben and Woodbridge, or south down to Maldon and the Blackwater. It's also an easy haul across to Holland with its extensive canal system.   The Pin Mill Sailing Club has a special relationship with the Dutch port town of Goes. Twenty-six years ago there was a move in the town to fill in their little harbour and turn it into a car park. Pin Mill wrote strongly in support of those who were against the idea and the plan was abandoned. Since then the Pin Mill Sailing Club has been invited over to Goes every year, and the annual visit of more than a dozen of their yachts is one of their most popular special events.

IN THE DAWN LIGHT THE ANNUAL PIN MILL SAILING
CLUB BARGE MATCH IS UNDERWAY

The Pin Mill Sailing Club was founded in 1936, which in one sense makes it the oldest club on the river. The Royal Harwich Yacht Club at Wolverstone is much older, but didn't actually move from Harwich on to the Orwell until the war years. It has seen life on the river change, starting with the boom in leisure sailing in the fifties when it would have been rare to see a twenty-eight foot yacht on the river. Now that's more the average with some yachts reaching well over thirty feet and even as much as forty feet. 'There's a lot of pressure on the river now,' Jeremy admitted. 'There's been a big increase in pleasure and commercial traffic, but we generally all get along together very well.'

Jeremy acknowledges that Pin Mill isn't as convenient for getting from yacht to shore and lacks some of the amenities of the more modern marinas, but that is reflected in lower subscription costs. The club knows its niche and Pin Mill is without doubt the most picturesque spot on the river.

WOOLVERSTONE MARINA, HOME OF THE ROYAL HARWICH YACHT CLUB

As the home of traditional sailing on the Orwell it is also host to the annual Thames Barge Match, which has been going on for over 40 years. 'They like coming here because we're a bit laid back,' Tony comments. 'They say they come for the racing but there's some pretty good apres-racing here in the clubroom 'We have over 400 members,' Jeremy added, 'and some of those are long standing members who go back over fifty years.'

We watched a white-sailed yacht go by, seeming to drift lazily up the river. Small boats dotted the moorings, contrasting with the exposed sea-faring debris around the old hulks on the mudflats.

I began to wish I owned a boat.

REMINDER, BUILT OF STEEL BY HORLOCKS OF MISTLEY IN 1929, STARTED HER RACING RECORD BY WINNING BOTH THE THAMES AND MEDWAY MATCHES IN THE SAME YEAR

RED SAILS ON THE ORWELL 15

15 RED SAILS ON THE ORWELL

It was a fine and pleasant day and they came down the Orwell in magnificent procession, their rust-brown sails taut and filled with the crisp morning breeze. They sailed in tight-packed groups, battling for wind and position. First the Class A bowsprits, *Gladys*, *May*, *Xylonite*, *Adieu*, *Edme* and *Mirosa*. Next the Class B staysails, *Cabby*, *Marjorie*, *Thistle*, *Reminder*, *Wyvenhow*, *Repertor* and *Phoenician*. And finally *Betula* and *Centaur*, the Class C staysails. This was the 40th anniversary of the Annual Pin Mill Barge Match and they were a splendid sight to see.

In the 1870s, at the peak of the barge trade, there would have been up to two thousand of these grand old sailing barges working in and out of our east coast ports, but now there are only thirty or so still afloat. They are a vital part of our traditional maritime heritage, kept alive by the love and dedication of their owners and skippers, and by the thrill of barge racing on the Thames and on the Medway, on the Colne and on the Blackwater, but most of all along the Orwell.

I was on board the motor boat *Gamine*, courtesy of her skipper Fiona Wiley and the Pin Mill Sailing Club. We had sailed from Shotley to meet the barges as they sailed down river, and the heeling sails stretched almost from shore to shore in saw-toothed ribbons of straining canvas. Skillfully Fiona took us around and behind the racing vessels for the best camera shots, as close as possible without getting in their seaway or their wind.

THE CLASS B STAYSAILS MAKING WAY DOWNRIVER

It was an exhilarating June morning, and the excitement of the race was contagious. We were almost a part of it as we held alongside the surging black hulls, close enough to count the knots on the rigging. We followed them back up to Shotley Point, past the towering cranes of Felixstowe docks and watched them head out into the North Sea.

They were due back at 5pm and the overall winner and first home in her Class was *Xyonolite*, built in 1926 by the Mistley ship-building company. *Betula*, built in 1924 was the first Class C staysail to sail triumphantly back into her home port. The Class B winner was the veteran *Marjorie*, a very familiar vessel in these waters, built at the Dock End Yard in Ipswich in 1902 and the only barge still sailing to have taken part in the very first Orwell Barge Race in 1962.

PHOENICIAN, CABBY AND *MARJORIE*, ALL BATTLING FOR THE WIND

It was a superb day of sailing with some wonderful skills and seamanship on display, and later I talked to Officer of the Day Mick Lungley to find out more about the background of the barge trade and barge racing on the Orwell. Mick first went to sea in 1952, first as mate and then as skipper of the *Venture*, a barge now long departed, although her transom still hangs on the wall of the Venture Pub in Chelmondiston. There would only be two men to crew a barge, Mick recalled. It was hard work, but with two men who knew what they were doing the work would be done almost automatically, 'almost as easy as driving a car.'

They carried flour from Cranfield's of Ipswich to Southwark and had to lower the mast to get under the Thames bridges. The mast would have to be raised again in order to get the hatches off to unload and then lowered again to get back downriver. Mick was with the *Venture* for five years or so, and was then skipper of the *Marjorie*. He moved from barges to coasters on the Baltic runs, and yet his heart was always with barges. He came ashore in 1981 and in 1985 took over the Limeburners pub at Often.

The barges had now finished their working lives. They had become too slow and uneconomic and those that survived had moved into the new leisure world of private charter. They also survived, and maintained the interest of the public at large, through racing and for the last twenty-eight years Mick has kept up his association with the barge world as Officer of the Day for the Orwell barge match. 'There were always annual barge matches on the Thames,' Mick explained, 'and after the Second World War they revived the Thames Barge races again in Coronation year. I sailed on the Thames race in the following year on the *Memory*, and I've been hooked on barge racing ever since.'

Mick's job as Officer of the Day is to set the course. There are twelve courses to choose from, ranging from just under eighteen miles to nearly thirty miles. The race always starts from Pin Mill at around nine o'clock in the morning, or as near as the tide will allow, and the aim of the race is for the barges to be back at the start line by five p.m. This is where all Mick's personal skills and experience comes into play. He has to take into account the nature of the tides, wind speeds and weather conditions, to decide which of the twelve possible courses will test the barges to give the best possible race on that particular day.

'We have a briefing the night before the race,' Mick explained. 'We study the weather forecast, and someone from Harwich Harbour Port Control will tell us what ships are in harbour and what the shipping movements will be, but we can't make the final decision on the course until the actual morning of the race. That's when I have to put my head on the block and make my choice.

THE *MARJORIE*, A FAMILIAR BARGE ON THE ORWELL,
ONCE SKIPPERED BY THE NOW OFFICER OF THE DAY, MICK LUNGLEY

'Down the river the course is always basically the same, and it's after they leave the river mouth that things have to vary. I have to make up my mind right at the start what the conditions will be like when they get out into the North Sea. If it's a calm day I can't send them too far because without wind they'll run out of time before they can get back. If I send them against the ebb tide that's fine until they get out of the river, but then they'll lose time because the ebb is running north and they'll hardly be able to move. If I send them to run down with the tide, then they've got to turn round and get back.'

We were studying the map of the river mouth and Mick pointed out where two of the courses were almost identical. 'The only difference is whether I turn them round the left or right hand side of the outer mark. I can send them round head to wind, or they can jibe round it. But if they jibe round and it's rough out there and there's a lot of wind, then they can do themselves a bit of damage. I did have to finish them once at the Outer Ridge, because one boat got fouled and had to be towed back.'

'Have you ever had to cancel a race ?' I asked him. 'Never,' he replied cheerfully. 'But we did have one year when the weather blew so hard that I couldn't send them out to sea, so I sent them up the Stour. But that's only a last resort because it's never a good race when you have to put a loop in the course. The leading barge might make the turn and get away from the rest because he's carrying the wind, but most of them will get bunched up and they'll all be blocking each other's wind.'

'Then you've got the risk of a collision, which is the last thing we want. Repair work is very expensive and it can put a barge out of action. We have had one or two knocks, a change in the wind and the barge won't come round, or comes too fast, that sort of thing. But nothing too serious. These skippers are all very experienced. They know what their barge is capable of, and they can see what's likely to happen so they're always ready for it.'

The rules are simple, any barge which detours from the set course, even by passing a marker buoy on the wrong side, is disqualified. Any barge which has to use her engines is disqualified. It's all down to sail and seamanship, and getting back over the finish line before the time limit.

'We don't get any problems with the commercial traffic,' Mick continued. 'The main thing is we talk to them. There's good communication over the radio between skippers and pilots. We let the pilots know when we're starting and they'll hold back a little bit. We did have one foreign ship come right through the start line one year and caused a bit of a kerfuffle. He couldn't make out what all the boats were doing.'

MAY, ON THE HOME RUN, PASSING PIN MILL

We browsed through some of his old race programmes, stirring up memories of old barges that are no longer sailing. 'Some of them come and go in the races as they change owner-ship.' Mick noted. 'A barge needs regular maintenance and that costs a lot of money. They have to come out of the water every year to be cleaned up. The amount of barnacles that can grow on them is unbelievable. Sometimes when the owners can't afford the maintenance they start falling into decline and that's when we lose them.'

Fortunately the handful that remain have a new lease of life, thanks to their charter work and they do take charter passengers on the annual round of barge racing. There will usually be fifteen or sixteen of these gallant old vessels racing on every annual barge race, which means that one Saturday in every July the Orwell will again be filled with the creaking of timber and rigging, the plunging black bows slicing the waters, and a skyline of straining, wind-blown sails.

May the days dawn fine and the winds blow fresh for all who sail in them.

THE SUFFOLK SHORE

16

16 The Suffolk shore

The coastline of Suffolk which the Romans found when their war galleys first began to explore our Saxon shore, just over two thousand years ago, was very different from the coastline we know today. The map with which we are familiar shows East Anglia as a smoothly rounded shoulder hunching out into the North Sea, as though the past two centuries of storm and tempest have filed the land into a more uniform shape. However, what Caesar's expeditionary forces discovered was a more ragged shoreline of deep sea creeks and estuaries in between far protruding headlands and islands.

LOWESTOFT HARBOUR, WITH THE LIFEBOAT AND THE *LYDIA EVA*,
THE LAST OF THE OLD EAST COAST STEAM DRIFTERS

Where Lowestoft is now there was an island called Lothingland, sitting at the mouth of a great molar shaped estuary that reached up deep into Norfolk and deep down into Suffolk. A conjectural map in Wilfred J Wren's excellent *Ports Of The Eastern Counties* shows four more deep inlets between Lothingland and Dunwich, and another at Aldeburgh. The Deben, and especially the Orwell, also provided deep sea lanes into the heart of the county.

Aldeburgh was originally a Roman settlement and may still have been an island in the Alde estuary, and Dunwich was most probably a Roman port. However, this wild land of the Iceni with its ragged and not particularly hospitable shore seemed to hold limited interest to the Romans. Apart from Dunwich, and a couple of defensive forts at Walton and Lothingland, the Suffolk coast was mainly by-passed. After 400 years of occupation the legions marched off to more urgent business at home and left Suffolk pretty much as they found it.

With the Romans gone our deeply indented coastline and the lush river valleys of the Orwell and the Deben proved much more attractive to the migrating waves of Angles and Saxons, who came over to settle from Europe. Ipswich was probably the first new town to be built by the Anglians, and the first Saxon settlements appeared at the head of the Deben at what is now Woodbridge. It was here that one powerful Anglo-Saxon group was to develop into the war-like Kingdom which ruled much of East Anglia during the 6th Century AD. Their kings were buried at Sutton Hoo.

The ferocious Vikings found rich pickings when their invasions began in the 9th Century. The developing ports of Ipswich, and probably Dunwich were prime targets. There were also thriving ports at Orford, Blythburgh and Southwold. The dreaded longships bearing down on the coastal ports, or pulling hard up the Orwell, were the first portent of terror, rape and plunder. Many attacks were simply pirate raids, but in 865 the Scandinavian Great Army landed and overran the whole of East Anglia.

King Alfred of Wessex finally defeated the Danes in 878, although the last Danish raid on Dunwich was not recorded until 1069. By then the Norman Conquest had taken place and in the relative stability that followed Dunwich and all the other ports grew rapidly. The herring shoals appeared regularly off the Suffolk coast, and there was rich fishing for the ships from all the Suffolk ports. Those great estuaries reaching inland around Lothingland had obviously dried out and silted up, and since late Anglo Saxon times the upper village of Lowestoft had also started developing as a thriving fishing community on the northern side of the river valley that remained.

By the early 13th Century Dunwich was the sixth greatest town and port in England, and in fierce competition with its neigh-bours at Blytheburgh and Walberswicke on the opposite side of the great estuary. Ships were built and owned at all three ports and the rights of trade and taxes were hotly disputed. Nature and the elements fuelled the grievances as the great shingle spit across the mouth of the estuary gradually extended to cut off Dunwich. New channels were cut to give continued access but eventually Dunwich was blocked by the great pile up of silt and shingle, and could only be reached by an inland estuary running behind the barrier from the mouth of the Blythe River. Eventually that too was blocked, Dunwich was doomed, but Blytheburgh, Walberswicke and Southwold prospered from its demise. Blytheburgh later followed Dunwich into decline as the Blythe Estuary shrank to the present narrow river of today, but in it's prime as a mediaeval port it accumulated enough wealth to build the magnificent Church of the Holy Trinity, which still stands high and proud as the Cathedral of the Marshes.

The final tragedies for Dunwich were the two great storms of 1287 and 1328. More than any other part of the Suffolk coastline Dunwich had always suffered from the relentless battering of the tides and the sea, and the slow erosion of its cliffs and the silting up of its harbour was nothing new. Over the past thousand years the whole coastline had been slowly changing as estuaries filled and headlands were eroded away. But the great storms were catastrophic, each one took great bites out of the harbour and cut great slices from the town itself. Ships were smashed and mangled at their moorings, and churches, windmills, homes and other buildings all went crashing down with the cliff-face into the sea. It was as though gigantic axe blades of wind and rain had simply chopped the town away.

WALBERSWICKE, STILL A PICTURESQUE HARBOUR FOR SMALL CRAFT

Despite the loss of Dunwich, and the gradual silting up of other harbours and erosion of the coastline, the Suffolk ports were generally thriving throughout the Middle Ages. Ipswich, Woodbridge, Walberswicke, and Dunwich and Blytheburgh in their heyday, all built warships for a succession of English kings, either to patrol the coastline against pirates and raiders or to take part in the seemingly endless wars against France. The building and out-fitting of warships and merchant ships was a thriving industry, and after the discovery of the Americas, Ipswich became a major centre for emigration to the New World.

England was now a major maritime trading nation and Ipswich became the dominant port. Lowestoft to the north rose to become the major Suffolk player in the herring fishery. During the 18th Century the coastline in between became a playground for smugglers, with contraband goods being run ashore on the beaches and off-loaded on to horse-drawn carts which could be brought down tracks through the dunes to the sea's edge. The doughty Suffolkmen who made their living from the sea could always turn their hand to something when the herring shoals were out of season, and out-witting the revenue men had always seemed a fair enough game.

Now everything has changed again. There is no more ship-building and no more of the great silver harvest from the herring. The Roman Saxon Shore has become the Suffolk Sunrise coast, a magnet for holiday makers and weekend sailors. Lowestoft has developed into a modern seaside resort, with its harbour filled with mainly pleasure craft and oil rig support vessels. However, in recent years Lowestoft has been holding an annual Fish Fayre in remembrance of it's glorious maritime heritage. It's a fund-raising festival in aid of the Royal National Mission to Deep Sea Fisherman, when the old Fish Dock comes alive again with resident and visiting trawlers, fishing smacks and barges. Shantymen bawl the old sail-raising and anchor-winding choruses on the quay. Many of the larger ships are open to the public, and the smaller sailing craft tack and circle round the inner harbour in a moving display.

Southwold is a more sedate resort, sharing its old harbour with Walberswicke on the opposite side of the Blythe River. The tall white tower of the lighthouse rises above the town and looks out over Sole bay where in 1672 a dawn to dusk naval battle was bitterly fought between the combined British and French and the Dutch Fleets. It was one of several sea battles over the trade and fishery rights in these lucrative waters. Below the lighthouse is Gun Hill, where six Elizabethan culverins can still be found with their black cannon barrels pointing out to sea.

The lighthouse from Gun Hill was the stock picture of Southwold, but now there is a better view from the smart new pier that was officially opened in 2001. The original pier was the landing stage for the old Belle steamers that brought holiday makers to Southwold in Victorian times, but the T end of the pier was swept away in a tumult of wind and waves in a savage storm in 1934. Now the view from the new pier, across the beach to the town, with the lighthouse behind and a row of those famous, multi-coloured beach huts before, must surely be the new number one postcard of Southwold. With perhaps Britain's last ocean-going paddle steamer, the *Waverly*, which now occasionally visits the new landing stage at the T end, becoming a close second.

The walk along the river at Walberswicke is still one of the most picturesque strolls in Suffolk, an ever-changing vista of charmingly rickety boat landings and jetties stretching out from the mud banks, with the river filled with both pleasure and working boats. Further inland all that remains of Blytheburgh's past glory is that huge and spectacular church.

The old port of Dunwich is all swallowed up by the sea. The gateway, part of the perimeter wall, and the ruins of the old Greyfriars Abbey being virtually all that remain, waiting their turn to be claimed by the next great storm to slice a chunk off the cliff face. There is a museum there telling the Dunwich story, but for a fully detailed account try reading *The Lost City Of Dunwich,* by Nicholas Comfort.

FISHING BOATS ON THE SHINGLE, ALL THAT REMAINS OF MARITIME ALDEBURGH

Further down the coast is Aldeburgh, another slightly genteel resort, with a long, steeply shelved shingle beach. It too was a busy fishing and ship-building centre in its mediaeval hey-day, and still has a busy lifeboat station, but now much of Aldeburgh has also been washed away. The relentless sea has stealthily advanced, and the lovely 15th Century timber and red brick Moot Hall that is Aldeburgh's premier heritage building, once sited in the centre of the town, now stands just above the shingle, only yards from the hungry waves.

Ipswich still has a busy working dock, but the mainstream of commercial sea traffic now flows in through the great container port at Felixstowe on the mouth of the Orwell. Built on reclaimed marshland at the end of the 19th Century the dock area seems to be in a continuous happy state of growth and expansion. There is a small car park and scenic viewpoint at Landguard Point, squeezed between the docks and the massive brick redoubt of Landguard Fort, and from here you can watch the passing sea traffic between Felixstowe and the rest of the globe, and between the opposite Essex port of Harwich and the key ports of Europe.

Landguard Fort has stood sentinel over the double mouth of the Stour and the Orwell since the 18th Century. An earlier fort was constructed in the 1540s and was attacked in 1667 by an invasion force of over 1,000 Dutch soldiers. The attack was twice repelled by stiff resistance from the defenders of the fort and from the Suffolk Militia fighting along the Felixstowe cliffs, and finally the enemy was forced to withdraw. It was the last time that an enemy force attempted to invade England, although the present fort has guarded against that threat through two world wars.

Felixstowe itself was only a small fishing village until the coming of the railway turned it into an Edwardian seaside resort. The pleasant little town is built on terraces along and above the cliffs, with a two mile promenade, a pier and a wide shingle beach. Once there was a priory and a Norman Castle here at Walton built, it is said, on the site of that old Roman fort, but all of that, like most of Dunwich, has long since vanished into the relentless sea.

WOODBRIDGE, STILL A BUSY LITTLE HARBOUR

So, it seems, that if any of those ancient centurions and soldiers could come back they would no longer recognise the terrain and shoreline where they once marched and conquered, and the erosion of Suffolk's coastline continues. In living memory, in 1953, high tidal surges and storms caused catastrophic floods, and cost hundreds of lives. The struggle to build sea defences goes on, and yet year by year more chunks of our coastline fall into the ever-hungry sea. Last year saw more extensive flooding, caused by heavy rainfall and global warming. The story is not yet finished and it seems inevitable that more and more of our Saxon Shore will be devoured by storm and tempest and a slowly rising sea level.

Perhaps we are fortunate to live now, and to know Suffolk as the lovely and peaceful county it is today.

SUMMER SHOWTIME

17

17 SUMMER SHOWTIME

The merry month of May, when Spring is in the air and summer on the way, is when Suffolk wakes up and starts to play. The Morris dancers appear, and from May to September you will find them outside pubs, on village greens, at folk fairs and at a whole variety of festivals. With feet flying, bells jingling, thwacking sticks or waving handkerchiefs, they will be whirling and weaving in circle and line dances that have come from the pre-Christian mists of pagan Britain. The dances are celebrations of the cycle of the seasons, for hunting and fishing, of Spring and Harvest, of fertility rites and rites of passage that are as ancient as Stonehenge and the Druids.

In their colourful and flamboyant costumes they keep ancient traditions alive in a feast of noisy music and dance that is joyful and vigorously energetic. At my last count there were some twenty Morris sides active and performing around Suffolk, all male sides, all female sides, and mixed. They have strangely exotic names like Barley Brigg, Little Egypt, Danegeld, Devil's Dyke, Gyppeswyck Garland, Haganeth, Green Dragon, the Haughley Hoofers, and the Leaping Ladies of Bury Fair. That is to name just a few. Find one of their performances outside one of those lovely old thatched country pubs on any warm summer evening, almost anywhere in Suffolk, and you have found an evening of rare and convivial entertainment.

May and June are also the months for the annual County Agricultural Shows, and with three agricultural shows within the county borders, Suffolk is spoiled for choice. Each show is not only a comprehensive showcase for the life and work of the farming community, they are also the venue for some of the most spectacular live events presented for the entertainment of the general public.

SUFFOLK MORRIS
WITH GYPPESWYCK
GARLAND

The Suffolk Show has been running since the 1840s and takes place over two days, usually in early June, at the Suffolk Showground in Ipswich. It will judge around 500 different livestock classes and usually attracts around 85,000 visitors.

DRAY HORSES ARE
A MAGNIFICENT
SIGHT AT ANY
AGRICULTURAL
SHOW

The South Suffolk Show has several times shifted its venue since it began running in 1888, but now has its regular home at Ampton near Bury St. Edmunds, and also draws huge crowds. The Hadleigh Agricultural Show is the smallest of the three, held annually at Holbecks Park near Hadleigh, and that too has a long history going back over 160 years.

At all three shows you will see exhibitors parading prize live-stock, horses, cattle, pigs, sheep and goats, all competing for the judge's eye and those highly coveted red, blue, and white rosettes. Every farmer wants to breed a champion. There is also a wide variety of equestrian events, possibly show-jumping, or pony and trap parades, or parades of heavy horses. A pair of magnificent Suffolk punches harnessed to a gleaming and perfectly restored brewer's dray wagon is a nostalgic sight not to be missed.

At either of the two larger shows you may see the dazzling acrobatics of motorcycle display teams, parachute freefall teams dropping out of the skies, pipe bands marching, armoured knights jousting, Roman chariots racing, or a Shetland Pony Grand National. All these events have been featured in recent years. The year 2000 highlight of the South Suffolk Show was the thrilling musical ride of the Household Cavalry. The riders, drawn from the mounted squadrons of the Life Guards and the Blues and Royals, gave a splendid display combining military precision and perfect horsemanship.

Another highly popular event in the Suffolk country calendar is the annual Euston Rural Pastimes Fair. Held in spacious Euston Park against the magnificent backdrop of 17th Century Euston Hall, the fair is an unparalleled Suffolk showcase of all those past arts and crafts and interests that were once centre stage of almost all rural life.

The show was first evolved as a fund-raising event for the local church, but has proved so successful that it still goes on, and is still raising money for local charities. The initial aim was to provide two days of summer fun for all the family, with tractor rides around the park and farm, a rally of vintage cars, tractors, motorcycles and steam engines, dog shows, displays of horses, ponies and farm animals, and any other suitable country activity that could be arranged. However, always at the core of the show is its fascinating range of rural craft demonstrations.

AT EUSTON FAIR,
CRAFTSMAN
JOE BERENS
DEMONSTRATES
THE ART OF
MAKING HURDLES

At my last visit I talked to a coppice craftsman and hurdlemaker
and learned that there can be over 200 different products from
a coppice, and that each type of wood has a different use; ash
for gate hurdles, hazel for windbreaks and sheepholding pens,
oak for fencing. Nearby was a craftsman hand-carving wooden
walking sticks, a task which could take from an hour to a week,
although the wood needed at least two years to season properly
before it was used. His choice woods were hazel, blackthorn,
ash and holly.

Other crafts being demonstrated were basket-making and thatching. The latter still a thriving business in a county with so many lovely old thatched cottages. There was a blacksmith and a beekeeper, and a gentleman making Victorian wheel-barrows. Farriers were bending horseshoes over ancient anvils. In the shade of a huge oak tree was a shepherd deftly shearing sheep. This was a hands on demonstration with members of the public being cheerfully invited to step up and have a go.

STEAM ENGINES ARE A POPULAR SIGHT AT AGRICULTURAL SHOWS

Suffolk in summer is also a paradise for gardeners, not only does every public park and town centre seem to be awash with colour, but private gardens everywhere are alive with roses, hollyhocks, petunias, and every blossom you can think of. Honeysuckle finds its scented golden way over every other wall and outhouse. And in many of the towns and villages, Bury St. Edmunds, Lavenham, Chelmsford and Walsham-le-Willows, there are Open Days when normally unseen private gardens will be thrown open to visitors.

Again these are fund-raising days for local causes and charities, and the purchase of a combined programme and map is also your entrance ticket to the whole range of gardens open for the day. They usually number from 25 to 30 gardens, a comfortable afternoon's walk around a village or town centre, and open up scores of horticultural delights, each one a secret oasis of flowers and greenery. You can find walled town gardens, tiny patios and courtyards, or, behind some of the larger houses, surprisingly expansive sweeps of lawns, shrubberies and orchards. Many of them incorporate water features, sundials and statues, and can range from a few yards square to half an acre, all of them lovingly tended and imaginatively designed.

For the keen gardener who may want to pick up a few tips, and for the casual visitor who just wants to enjoy the charm and beauty of these hidden havens, an Open Gardens day is an excellent day out. All the host gardeners will be happy to advise and explain, and somewhere along the route teas and home-made cakes will almost certainly be provided for refreshment.

Among the more unusual annual Suffolk attractions is the crab-catching competition at Walberswicke, where thousands of eager children and their parents will be found dipping their hand nets into mud pools and the river. There are usually a few enthusiasts along the quay and riverbank at any time, but on competition day they are there in an excited multitude.

The Westleton Barrel Fair is another annual event that should not be missed. A serious test of skill, luck and nerve, the barrel racing takes place on the large village green, where lines of hay bales mark out the sides and bottom end of the 100 yard course. The green is on a steep slope and the competitors come hurtling down it at break-neck speed, using five foot poles to prod and pursue the full size, bouncing metal beer barrels. Like out of control cannon balls the barrels will leap, twist and spin in the sunlight. The aim is to control the barrels by pushing them dead centre with the poles, but any misjudgement can send the slightly ovoid barrels spinning off at a tangent, and even those who successfully master the right technique can still fall foul of the unexpected bump or rut in the grass.

AT WESTLETON THE BARREL RACING IS OPEN TO ALL, HERE A GIRL
LEADS THE FIELD OF BOYS IN ONE OF THE JUNIOR RACES

You can pick out the beginners to this hilarious sport because they are usually in the lead on the downhill run. The haybale barrier stops them from flying straight into the duckpond beyond, but as they turn to make the return uphill run to the finish line they are immediately faced with the daunting spectacle of the rest of the field still thundering towards them. That's when the barrels smash and collide and all planned strategies go completely out of control. However, it is all great fun.

To return to the sane but spectacular, there is always the annual Bury Balloon Festival, held at Rougham Airfield just outside Bury St. Edmunds. The highlights here are the inflation and ascent of up to a score of vividly colourful hot air balloons, and later the night glow finale when the tethered balloons are brilliantly illuminated by alternating hot-air bursts in time to a programme of classical music.

Some of the large commercial balloons can be up to 250,000 cubic feet in canopy size, with a basket that can carry up to a dozen passengers. I was fortunate enough to be given a flight in Dugi-G, a chequered red, white, blue and yellow canopy, with a 90,000 cubic feet hot air capacity, and a basket to carry three. We were the fourth to inflate in the mass lift off, so that as we ascended there were balloons above and below, quickly filling the skies on all horizons.

It was a magical experience, drifting through a perfectly calm and mellow summer evening with a silver mackerel sky that eventually flushed into sunset red. The white sails of Pakenham windmill far below helped me to orientate our position as we passed over Thurston, Pakenham and Ixworth at 1400 feet. Floating at this height all was silent, beautiful and peaceful, with the pastoral loveliness of Suffolk spread out in patchwork fields and woodlands of green and gold between the shadow-blurred edges of the curved earth. Then Dougie Cook, my pilot, brought us down to sail just inches above the tops of the golden cornfields, skimming hedgerows, vineyards and a copse of fir trees. The hour-long flight was all too quickly over and we landed gently as a kiss in a stubble field near Stanton.

THE MAGICAL, MUSICAL NIGHTGLOW FINALE AT
THE BURY ST. EDMUNDS BALLOON FESTIVAL

There are other regular events at Rougham, the annual Wings,
Wheels and Steam flying display of small aircraft, and an annual
Kite Festival. Lowestoft also has an annual Air Show. Woodbridge has an annual Horse Show. Woolpit has an annual Steam
Engine Rally. Bury St. Edmunds has a two-week Music Festival
every May, and almost every major town and resort has its annual
summer carnival or regatta. To find out exactly what is on and
when it is only necessary to pay a visit or to make a telephone
call to any Tourist Information Centre.

Suffolk is a truly wonderful county in which to live, to explore,
and to enjoy yourself.

All of the chapters in this book first appeared as feature articles in Suffolk's premier county magazine, The Suffolk Journal. This glossy monthly magazine combines a fascinating range of modern lifestyle features with a mix of beautifully illustrated photo features covering Suffolk's heritage, Suffolk places, Suffolk events and Suffolk people. Published by Acorn Magazines Limited, from Bury St. Edmunds in the heart of the county, the Suffolk Journal can be found on all major news-stands.

For more insights into Suffolk, and a regular arts update and news of events, why not try a copy. The monthly Robert Leader Where in Suffolk Quiz gives the opportunity to win a free twelve months subscription, and if you can't wait to win, it's easy enough to subscribe anyway.

Contact The Suffolk Journal at:
The Old County School
Northgate Street
Bury St. Edmunds
Suffolk IP33 1HP
Tel: 01284 701190

TOURIST INFORMATION OFFICES IN SUFFOLK

Bury St Edmunds
6 Angel Hill, Bury St. Edmunds, IP33 1UZ
Tel: 01284 757084

Ipswich
St. Stephen's Church, St. Stephens Lane, Ipswich, IP1 1DP
Tel: 01473 258070

Lavenham
Lady Street, Lavenham, CO10 9RA
Tel: 01787 248207

Felixstowe
Seafront, Felixstowe, IP11 8AB
Tel: 01394 276770

Lowestoft
East Point Pavilion, Royal Plain, Lowestoft, NR33 OAP
Tel: 01502 523000

OTHER THOROGOOD TITLES

A TASTE OF WARTIME BRITAIN

Edited by Nicholas Webley

£9.99 paperback, published in 2003

A vivid and evocative collection of eye-witness accounts, diaries, reportage and scraps of memory from people who lived through the dark days of World War II. Lavishly illustrated with many newspaper pictures and personal photos, the book shows what life was like for millions of ordinary people throughout the war – men, women, children, soldiers and civilians. It brilliantly captures the sights, the smells and sounds and the voices of a country at war.

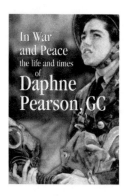

IN WAR AND PEACE – THE LIFE AND TIMES OF DAPHNE PEARSON GC

An autobiography

£17.99 cased, published in 2002

Daphne Pearson, born in 1911, was the first woman to be given the George Cross, it was awarded for acts of courage in circumstances of extreme danger. This is the inspiring story of a very courageous and remarkable woman.

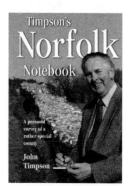

TIMPSON'S NORFOLK NOTEBOOK

John Timpson

£9.99 paperback, published in 2002

A collection of renowned writer and broadcaster John Timpson's best writing about Norfolk, its ancient and subtle landscape, places with strange tales to tell, remarkable and eccentric people and old legends and traditions.

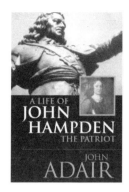

A LIFE OF JOHN HAMPDEN – THE PATRIOT

John Adair

£12.99 paperback, published in 2003

John Hampden, statesman and soldier, was a cousin to Oliver Cromwell and, had he not met an untimely death at the Battle of Chalgrove during the Civil World War in 1643, he might well have achieved similar fame in English history, both as a soldier and parliamentarian. This classic study of a great man has been out of print for some years and is now published in paperback for the first time.

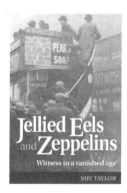

JELLIED EELS AND ZEPPELINS

Sue Taylor

£8.99 paperback, published in 2003

As every year goes by, the number of people able to give a first hand account of day-to-day life in the early part of the last century naturally diminishes. The small but telling detail disappears. Ethel May Elvin was born in 1906; she recalls her father's account of standing sentry at Queen Victoria's funeral, the privations and small pleasures of a working class Edwardian childhood, growing up through the First World War and surviving the Second. Anyone intrigued by the small events of history, how the majority actually lived day-to-day, will find this a unique and fascinating book.

CONFESSIONS OF A COUNTRY BOY

Keith Skipper

£8.99 paperback, published in 2002

Memories of a Norfolk childhood fifty years ago: this is broadcaster and humorist Keith Skipper in his richest vein, sharp and witty, occasionally disrespectful, always affectionate. As he says himself 'Distance may lend enchantment, but my country childhood has inspired much more than rampant nostalgia. I relish every chance to extol the virtues of a golden age when... life was quieter, slower, simpler...'

'He delights our days and does so much for Norfolk.'
Malcolm Bradbury

BETTY'S WARTIME DIARY – 1939-1945

Edited by Nicholas Webley

£9.99 paperback, published in 2002

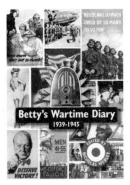

The Second World War diary of a Norfolk seamstress. Here, the great events of those years are viewed from the country: privation relieved by poaching, upheaval as thousands of bright young US servicemen 'invade' East Anglia, quiet heroes and small -time rural villains. Funny, touching and unaffectedly vivid.

'Makes unique reading... I am finding it fascinating.'
David Croft, co-writer and producer of BBC's hit comedy series 'Dad's Army'